THE
Outboard Motor
MANUAL

Other titles in the
Adlard Coles Nautical
Motorboats Monthly
series:

Starting Motorboating: Emrhys Barrell
This introductory book is aimed at newcomers to
motorboating seeking advice on the type of boat to
buy to suit their needs.

Practical Motor Cruising: Dag Pike
Dag Pike takes motor cruiser owners by the hand to
show them the ropes of *practical* motorboat handling
and management in harbour, on rivers and at sea.

Fast Boats and Rough Seas: Dag Pike
A more advanced follow up to *Practical Motor
Cruising*, designed to explain advanced handling
techniques for fast boats.

*Marine Inboard Engines:
Petrol and Diesel*: Loris Goring
This book will enable every owner to maintain their
diesel or petrol engine to maximise its lifespan and
avoid breakdown at sea.

Fast Boat Navigation: Dag Pike
Aimed at owners of all fast boats from 20 knot cabin
cruisers to racing powerboats, fast ferries, patrol boats
and lifeboats, this book provides a complete survey of
the environment and techniques of high speed
navigation.

*For more information on the above, contact
Adlard Coles Nautical at 35 Bedford Row,
London WC1R 4JH
or* Motorboats Monthly *at Link House,
Dingwall Avenue, Croydon, Surrey CR9 2TA.*

THE
Outboard Motor
MANUAL

Keith Henderson

ADLARD COLES NAUTICAL
London

05231312

Published by Adlard Coles Nautical
an imprint of A & C Black (Publishers) Ltd
35 Bedford Row, London WC1R 4JH

Copyright © Keith Henderson 1992

First published in Great Britain by
Adlard Coles Nautical

ISBN 0–7136–3424–3

A CIP catalogue record for this book is
available from the British Library.

Typeset in $10\frac{1}{2}/12\frac{1}{2}$pt Caledonia,
printed and bound in Great Britain by
J. W. Arrowsmith Ltd, Bristol

Contents

Acknowledgements

The illustrations and diagrams throughout this book have been kindly donated by Honda Marine Europe, Marine Power Europe, OMC Europe N V, Suzuki Motor Company, Yamaha Motor Europe, and Yanmar Diesel Engine Company. I would like to express my thanks to them, and to Castrol, E.P.Barrus, Indespension, and Lew-Ways, for their co-operation and assistance in providing information and illustrations for the book.

Introduction

In writing this book, I have kept uppermost in my thoughts the question of what a new owner needs to know about an outboard, both before and after purchase. Whether you are still in the process of looking for an outboard, or have just bought one and now want to make the best of your investment, *The Outboard Motor Manual* will guide you along the path.

For a newcomer to the world of outboard motors, the choice of models on offer is bewildering. Deciding which brand to choose may be difficult; which of the many models put out by each manufacturer to go for, even more so. Today's outboard industry is dominated by four manufacturers, two American and two Japanese, operating multinationally. Brunswick sell motors under the Mercury, Mariner and Force (formerly Chrysler) brand names, Outboard Marine the Evinrude and Johnson brands. Yamaha and Suzuki use their own names, although some Suzukis were sold in the USA as Spirit outboards.

The rest of the industry is led by Tohatsu, who also make some of the Nissan outboard range. Yanmar produce a line of diesel outboards, Honda a line of four-cycle models. In Europe Selva of Italy continues to market a range of outboards, as do the smaller British Seagull and—manufacturers of the only outboard to emerge from Eastern Europe in any quantity— Tomos of Yugoslavia. A few other independents produce specialist outboards on a relatively small scale.

With this wide choice in mind, *The Outboard Motor Manual* gives you all the information you need on the features manufacturers pack into each size of outboard, to make the job easier when deciding which features are really essential, which ones are 'nice to have', and which ones are best avoided.

The Outboard Motor Manual is intended not only as a book to be read from cover to cover, but also as a reference. With this in mind we have included an extensive index to speed up the search for the appropriate text. Where a subject needs to be discussed in more than one section, it may be covered more than once, so that each section is complete in its own right, and you shouldn't have to flick constantly from one part of the book to another.

Keith Henderson

1 What is an outboard?

THE BEGINNINGS OF OUTBOARD POWER

The history of the outboard motor begins some time before anyone had ever thought of the concept. The first outboard made its appearance a little more than a hundred years ago, but even then it represented the culmination of a series of inventions that went back much further to the dawn of powered craft.

In the early days of mechanical propulsion, boats simply used scaled-down versions of the steam-driven paddle systems that powered large ships. The first departure from steam was in 1838, when a Russian physicist called Professor Jacobi harnessed an electric motor to a set of paddle wheels. But paddle wheels were bulky and inefficient, and it was not until the invention of the screw propeller some years later that the innovators of the period woke to the possibility of producing a compact, self-contained method of propelling a boat through the water.

In 1866 T. Reece of Philadelphia patented a screw propeller. His invention, although a hand-driven affair relying on muscle power, laid down some design features that would be incorporated later into the outboard motor. It could be moved from one boat to the other, and was attached by screw clamps. It steered as well as providing thrust. The horizontal propeller shaft was driven by a vertical drive shaft, through a set of bevel gears, all still to be found in today's outboards.

Many variations on this theme followed, including pedal power, but fifteen years passed before anyone produced a working design using a machine to drive the Reece propeller. It was the Frenchman Trouvé who can claim to have been the founder of the outboard motor. His prototype 'Motor and Screw' was exhibited at the 1881 Paris Exhibition, powered by an electric motor driving the propeller via a chain. Several designs of electric-powered outboards followed in the forthcoming years, from inventors on both sides of the Atlantic.

The first petrol-powered outboard is reported to have made its appearance in 1896. Built by the American Motors Company of New York, the 544cc single-cylinder four-stroke engine developed between 1 and 2hp at a stately 400–600rpm.

This outboard was remarkable in other ways. The engine layout, with horizontal cylinder and vertical crankshaft, is the configuration still used in today's outboards. The tiller could not only be moved from side to side to steer, but also up and down to alter the pitch of the propeller: thus change of direction, forward or astern, could be achieved without the complication of a gearbox.

Of the many designs of outboards that followed, most of them remained mere designs, some reached prototype stage, and a very few were produced in commercial quantities. A century later, all the names of the pioneers of that era have passed into history, except one which is still with us today.

It was the enterprising Ole Evinrude who imagined that there were better ways of crossing Lake Okauchee in Wisconsin than rowing. Maybe the hot summer's day in 1906 added an incentive to his creativity—the story goes that he was trying to cross the lake with an ice cream for a lady; but whatever the truth, he subsequently spent much of his spare time working on his idea of a motor that could be attached to the stern of a rowing boat. Ole's prototype design was completed in 1907, and consisted of a horizontal cylinder, with vertical crankshaft, and a driveshaft with direction-changing gears housed in an underwater gear housing.

Evinrude's first outboards developed $1\frac{1}{2}$hp, and were sold locally to friends: orders soon flowed in from further afield and, on his wife's insistence, the Evinrude Motor Company was founded in Milwaukee, Wisconsin and the Evinrude marque was born.

THE QUEST FOR SPEED

It was the invention of the internal combustion engine in the latter part of the nineteenth century that heralded the birth of the motor boat. Steam yachts had been the preserve of the super-rich. Petrol power brought a new compactness and a new convenience to boating, and gradually quite ordinary people began boating for fun.

Human nature being what it is, as motor boats developed there was a continuing demand for ever higher speeds. This required a more subtle solution than simply fitting increasingly larger engines. The displacement boat hulls which were the standard of the day—and these are still the norm in most commercial vessels—become unstable when pushed faster and faster.

The problem was solved by the Polynesians, who have been racing over the seas in sail-driven craft for thousands of years. They couldn't just pour on more power, being entirely dependent on wind strength. The Polynesians' craft were fundamentally different from what we were used to: their boats skimmed, or planed, over the water surface rather than trying to cut through, or displace, the water.

To achieve high speeds, the boat hull must be designed for planing. For fast planing, as little of the hull as possible should be in contact with the water, because the water friction, or drag, slows the boat down. The designer therefore needs to think seriously about weight distribution—especially the not insignificant weight of engine and transmission.

In the case of the inboard engine, the further forward the engine is in the boat, the more the hull is pushed down in the water, increasing the wetted area and slowing the boat down. If the weight can be placed further aft, less of the hull will be in contact with the water and therefore the faster the boat will go (Figure 1a).

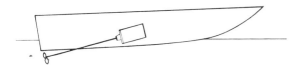

Fig. 1a. The smaller the wetted area, the faster a planing boat can go. This can be done by moving the weight aft.

Positioning the engine further aft leads to other problems because the angle to the horizontal increases to such a point that fuel or oil supply may be affected. Also, the angle of the shaft means that the propellers start losing efficiency (Figure 1b).

Fig. 1b. The steeper angle of engine and drive will affect performance.

One way round this problem is to use vee-drives (Figure 1c), popular with racing boats.

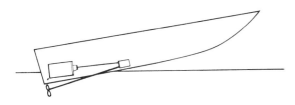

Fig. 1c. Vee-drives are designed to overcome this problem.

Another way is to move the engine so far aft that it is hanging out over the stern—as happens when you fit an outboard. The result will be a hull that can reach substantially higher speeds than it would be capable of with an inboard.

While on the subject of alternative engine layouts, it is worth briefly mentioning sterndrives. This is a cross between an inboard and an outboard (hence its alternative name of inboard/outboard), with an inboard engine coupled to an outdrive leg attached to the transom. The principle was established in 1892, when the Frenchman Alfred Seguin of Paris tested his prototype 'Motogodille', but the modern sterndrive was the brainchild of American Jim Wynne.

It was Volvo Penta who were the first to recognise the potential of Wynne's invention as a method of boat propulsion. Combining the advantages of both inboard and outboard, the sterndrive first appeared at the 1959 New York Boat Show, and grew to dominate the 18–35ft powerboat market.

Installation of a sterndrive is relatively simple. Its main weight and thrust are carried on the boat's transom, so that the hull does not need the substantial engine and transmission bearers required for an inboard installation. The usual shaft alignment problems thrown up by inboards are also reduced, if not eliminated altogether. Finally, unlike an inboard, a sterndrive limits the number of holes that have to be made in the hull to just one: transmission, water intake and exhaust all pass through one central aperture in the transom, to the drive unit.

In use, the sterndrive has several important advantages. Like the outboard, its drive unit tilts up if it hits a submerged object. Also like the outboard, the whole unit is supplied by one manufacturer, who is responsible for warranty and service matters.

The sterndrive, however, remains fundamentally an inboard engine with the inboard's associated disadvantages.

ADVANTAGES OF THE OUTBOARD

We have already explained how the position of the engine relative to the boat enables outboards to outperform inboard engines on boats with planing hulls. (In fact the outboard can be moved even further aft than the boat's transom by using special brackets which hold the outboard well clear of the stern, for even greater speed—these are more fully discussed in Chapter 3.)

There are many other features of the outboard worthy of consideration. It can be transferred to another boat without incurring major costs. Made of die-cast aluminium, it is substantially lighter than an equivalent inboard, which will be weighed down by a cast iron engine block, separate gearbox, thick stainless steel shafts, bearings, steering system and rudder. In fact, depending on your strength, outboards of up to about 25hp are portable.

The outboard also gives more room in the boat, as the whole engine is carried outside the hull (although most models above 5hp use a separate fuel tank which has to be stowed in the boat). It can be quieter, at least for the occupants of the boat: if you are using remote control steering, engine noise is less noticeable because you sit some way in front of the engine, instead of on or beside it as you would do with an inboard. Finally, transom bolts excepted, you don't need to make any holes in the hull to install the engine—so there's no chance of leakage.

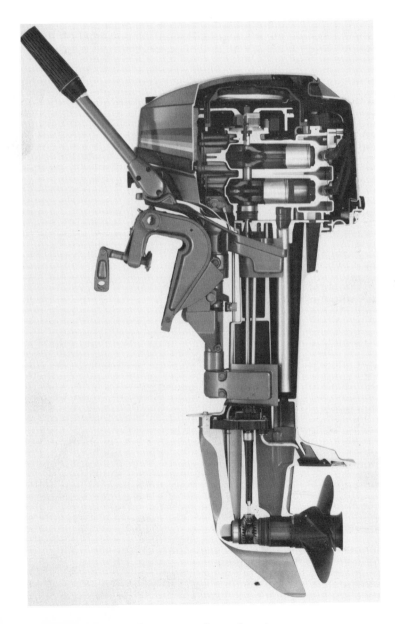

Fig. 2. A typical modern two-stroke outboard.

When launching from a ramp, an outboard-powered boat can be launched in shallower water than its inboard counterpart because the whole engine can be tilted up, in effect retracting the propeller. This means that the trailer doesn't need to go completely underwater, which avoids the risk of wheel bearing damage.

The greatest single advantage of the outboard over an inboard is its ability to swing up if it strikes a submerged object. Some outboard manufacturers even show a 'log test' in their promotional videos, in which an outboard-powered boat is driven at speed over a telegraph pole submerged just under the water surface. A degree of nerve is required for this manoeuvre because if the driver gets cold feet at the last minute and shifts into neutral when closing the throttle, the reverse lock can engage, preventing the outboard from tilting up, and smashing the lower unit!

A rather more common and gentler use of this feature is when running into shallow water or beaching. Running aground with an inboard will usually result in severe damage to the propeller, shaft and rudder, and may even rip them off completely.

Because an outboard is a complete self-contained propulsion unit, horsepower for horsepower it is very much cheaper than an inboard package consisting of engine, gearbox, stern tube, propeller shaft, shaft bearings and rudder.

An outboard leaves you with more choices when the time comes to sell the boat: you can sell the engine with the boat, or transfer it to your next one. You can also easily re-power with a different size of engine. With an inboard, the time and materials required for installation make both these options rather less attractive.

If anything goes wrong with an inboard, you will be faced with higher costs in removing the defective part from the boat. The mechanic may even have to come to the boat, whereas an outboard can usually simply be removed from the boat and taken to the service shop for repairs, servicing or winter storage.

OUTBOARD OR NOT?

An outboard is not the ideal engine for every use, but there are numerous areas in which it outperforms the alternatives. The list below grades outboard, inboard and sterndrive installations on a scale of 1 to 3 (1 is best, 3 worst).

	Outboard	Sterndrive	Inboard
Weight	1	2	3
Purchase price	1	2	3
Installation cost	1	2	3
Ease of launching/recovery	1	1	3

	Outboard	Sterndrive	Inboard
Running aground	1	1	3
Space saving	1	2	3
Ease of servicing	1	2	3
Reliability (petrol engine)	1	1	1
Running costs	3	1	1
Theft	3	1	1
Ease of replacement	1	2	3

OUTBOARDS: THE CHOICE

A convenient way of classifying the many types of outboard is by fuel type.

The smallest outboards are electrically powered. Most commonly used by sports fishermen (because of their silent operation), they are ideally suited to driving in shallow waters: being entirely pollution-free, they are steadily becoming more popular in other areas and are the only type of mechanical propulsion allowed on some lakes and reservoirs.

A large car or truck battery will usually give several hours' running time, depending of course on the speed. In the USA, electrics are used in combination with larger petrol-driven outboards of 100hp or more on bass boats (special sport fishing boats). The large outboard is used to get to the fishing grounds as fast as possible; it is then switched off, and the electric outboard is used to propel the boat quietly to where the sonar suggests fish can be found. This application is so refined that black or transparent propellers are available for electric outboards. The choice depends on which you think least frightens the fish!

Virtually unknown to the outboard world until 1988 was the diesel; then somewhat unexpectedly the Japanese engine manufacturer Yanmar introduced a diesel outboard. Up till then the only diesel outboards had been made in small quantities for specialist users by companies such as Ruggerini of Italy.

Diesel outboards, however, are really more suited to commercial use because they are much heavier than petrol models of equivalent power. They do use a less volatile fuel, which has safety advantages; also fuel consumption is lower, which, where annual running times are high (e.g. 12,000 hours), compensates for the diesel's higher initial cost. See Figure 3, overleaf. An additional bonus is the tax-free fuel on offer to professional users in many countries.

The outboard as we know it usually runs on petrol (gasoline), exceptionally on paraffin (kerosene). By far the majority of outboards have two-stroke (two-cycle) engines. In recent years there has been an increase in the number of four-stroke models available, the most popular being made by Honda and Yamaha.

Fig. 3. Comparison of outboards using different fuels.

Fuel type	Petrol	Diesel
Outboard model	Yamaha 25D	Yanmar 27
Power HP/rpm	25/5500	27/4500
Displacement (cc)	430	808
Weight lb (kg)	104 (47)	192 (87)
Fuel consumption lt/hr Imp galls/hr	12.0 2.64	6.8 1.59

Fig. 4. The Yanmar 27hp diesel outboard.

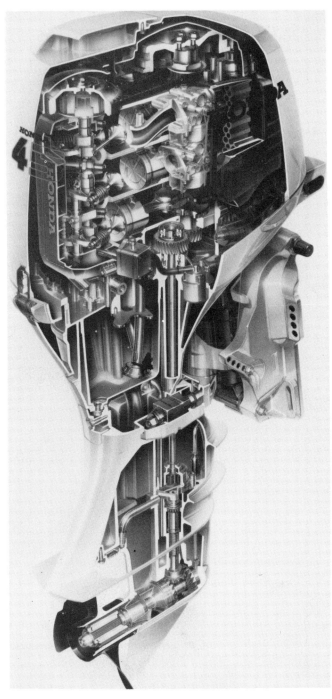

Fig. 5. The Honda 45 four-stroke outboard.

Honda, who until recently made a range that stopped at 20hp, are the first company to manufacture higher-powered four-stroke outboards designed for use on planing runabouts and cruisers since the 55hp Homelite/Bearcat 55 disappeared from the market in 1972. There is considerable interest by the major outboard manufacturers in four-stroke engines and it will probably not be long before more companies are offering four-strokes to complement their range of two-stroke models.

The advantages of the four-stroke outboard as compared with the two-stroke are its cleaner exhaust, smoother idle, and better fuel consumption. Against it can be ranged higher price, increased maintenance and greater weight. The advantage gained by using pure fuel (i.e. without pre-mix oil) has diminished over the years with the availability of automatic oil injection systems on most two-stroke outboards.

An unusual variant of the two-stroke is the paraffin-powered outboard. In some countries this fuel is available tax-free as TVO (Tractor Vaporising Oil), which makes it popular among professional users. Even outboards with outputs as low as 8hp run well on this fuel.

Referred to in most brochures as kerosene models, paraffin outboards are in fact dual-fuel engines, with special carburettors that feed the engine with pure petrol to start and idle, gradually switching over to almost pure paraffin at full throttle. The whole process functions automatically, and most models perform very well. That having been said, the demise of TVO in favour of diesel as a commercial fuel has reduced the availability of TVO to such an extent that it is often difficult to obtain. Paraffin for lighting and heating tends to be more expensive than petrol, so the paraffin outboard only remains popular where the fuel is available and is tax-free.

It is beyond the scope of this book to delve into the functioning of the internal combustion engine, as there are many excellent books around covering this topic in depth for readers sufficiently interested in the subject. Nevertheless, there is one attribute of the two-stroke outboard that is important to understand when buying an engine: the scavenging method used. There are two types, cross-flow and loop-charged.

Cross-flow scavenging produces smoother idling characteristics but produces less power per litre of engine capacity than loop-charged scavenging. It also uses slightly more fuel. The cross-flow is therefore more often to be found on small outboards where smooth idling outweighs the disadvantages.

Loop-charging is a later improvement on the traditional cross-flow scavenging system that was developed by a German engineer called Schnürle (hence its alternative name of Schnürle loop scavenging). It produces more power per litre of engine capacity than any other two-stroke scavenging system. Fuel consumption is also good, the main disadvantage being that the idle speed must be kept rather high, otherwise the 'loop' in the combustion chamber collapses, giving a rough idle or even stalling. This point has been the subject of considerable research effort, and its 'disadvantage' has been reduced to such an acceptable level that more and more new small outboards are using loop-charging.

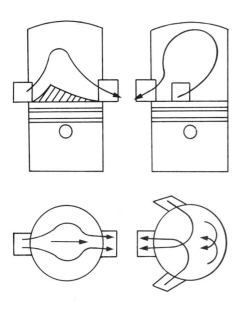

Fig. 6. Difference between cross-flow (left) and loop scavenging (right).

INSIDE THE OUTBOARD

Lubrication

The modern two-stroke engine generally has a lower tolerance than four-strokes to 'oil abuse', by which I mean using the wrong type of oil. It also has a lower tolerance than earlier two-strokes. Older outboard models were designed for, and could run on, a wide variety of oils from castor oil to old car engine oil, but such tolerance had a very high price, especially on the environment. Fuel/oil ratios of 10:1 were quite common, producing oil-fouled spark plugs, not to mention the clouds of blue smoke and trail of oil behind the boat! The 10:1 ratio was necessary to ensure that enough oil reached the surfaces requiring lubrication: that the rest of the oil was dumped overboard through leaking seals, or out through the exhaust, didn't seem to worry too many people in those days.

Now, special outboard oils have been developed so that fuel/oil ratios of 150:1 are permitted. Though kinder on the environment, this has limited your options: an engine designed to use a particular oil can be irreparably damaged if you use the wrong kind.

So that we can better understand what is so special about outboard oil, let us consider what it is expected to do. First, as with all two-stroke engines, the oil is carried to the parts requiring lubrication via the fuel. Consequently the oil has to mix easily with the fuel: if it doesn't, the oil will lie at the bottom of the fuel tank with the petrol on top, and sooner rather than later vital moving parts will be starved of oil, with inevitable costly damage.

Most of an outboard's life is spent stationary on the transom of a boat, in a moist salty atmosphere, the perfect conditions to corrode unpainted metal parts unless they are protected by a film of oil. This, then, is the oil's second function.

Thirdly, two-stroke outboard oil has to be relied upon to burn up completely in the combustion chamber. Unburnt oil deposits will foul the spark plugs or, worse, burnt oil deposits in the form of ash become so hot that they ignite the fresh mixture entering the combustion chamber before the spark plug has a chance to do its work (pre-ignition). This quickly leads to engine damage, such as holes in pistons.

Fourthly, outboard oil must be an excellent lubricant because outboards generally develop high engine powers from small-capacity blocks. Also, unlike most other engines, marine engines tend to be run for long periods at constant speeds, which in itself makes further demands on oil quality.

The traditional way of bringing the lubricating oil to the moving parts is by mixing it with fuel in the tank. Oil and fuel are then carried together in liquid form to the carburettor and reed valves, where the fuel is vaporised, leaving the oil deposited on the engine surfaces.

During the 1970s and 1980s all the major manufacturers introduced alternative, simpler ways of achieving this task. Although they all claim to offer oil injection, in fact the systems available fall into two classifications: true oil injection, and oil mixing, which in turn can be subdivided into variable-ratio mixing (VRM) and fixed-ratio mixing (FRM).

Oil injection systems pump oil from a separate oil tank which, depending on the outboard model, can be mounted either on the engine or in the boat. The oil is brought via gravity or a feed pump to the injection pump, which is usually mounted at the base of the engine and driven from the crankshaft. The pump unit distributes oil to the individual cylinders, also injecting it into the crankcase to ensure that the crankshaft bearings as well as the pistons receive adequate lubrication.

What makes this system unique is that the oil is squirted neat into the engine and the swirling air/fuel mixture carries the oil onto the engine surfaces. Because the pump is driven from the crankshaft, the amount of oil delivered is proportional to the engine speed and the throttle setting.

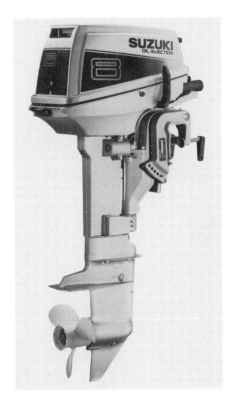

Fig. 7. One of the smallest outboards with standard oil injection, the Suzuki 8.

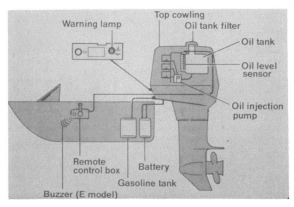

Fig. 8. Yamaha's Autolube oil injection system.

In this way the fuel/oil ratio varies from a lean 150:1 for light loading, e.g. at idle, right up to 50:1 under full power.

The oil mixing systems come in different forms. They all work on the same principle, however: oil is added to the fuel either at or before the carburettor, if a variable-delivery pump is used, or at the fuel tank or fuel line if the pump delivers a fixed ratio (Figure 9).

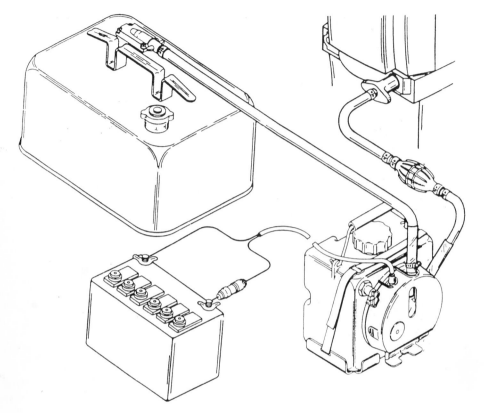

Fig. 9. The Mercury/Mariner Autoblend oil mixing system for smaller outboards.

Cooling

Although the idea of an air-cooled engine is attractive, because it does away with the need for a water pump, in practice air-cooled outboards have always had a measure of water cooling. The fan might be relied upon to cool the engine, but the exhaust tube always ran the risk of overheating. This would cause the lubricating grease round the steering collar to drip out, making the steering very heavy.

In most air-cooled units, therefore, the hottest part of the engine around the exhaust receives supplementary cooling via a pressure tube positioned behind the propeller. Using the thrust of the propeller, cooling water is forced up the tube to the engine, thereby removing the necessity for a water pump. Noise, and the quest for leaner fuel/oil levels with cooler-running engines, has virtually killed off the air-cooled outboard in favour of the full water-cooled variety.

Provided the water-cooled outboard is not abused, e.g. by running the engine dry, or not flushing it out with fresh water occasionally to prevent the build-up of salt deposits, the water pump will cope with its task very well. Unfortunately some owners like to 'fire up' their outboards on dry land, a practice that is guaranteed to burn up the impeller or plastic pump cover within 30 seconds. If the damaged pump isn't noticed, running the engine further in water will cause the engine to overheat and even lead to engine seizure—a very expensive experience. So **never** run an outboard on dry land.

Fig. 10. Water pump impellers: (bottom) 100 hours in water, (top) 100 seconds out of water!

Ignition systems

One of the greatest steps forward in the outboard motor's reliability has been the advent of high-energy electronic ignition systems. It has also allowed the introduction by some manufacturers of a new generation of spark plugs, surface gap spark plugs, which are impossible to foul. Over the last decade the use of the marine magneto has diminished, manufacturers steadily ousting the magneto in favour of electronic ignition systems as they bring out successive new models, until now only the smallest engines still use magnetos.

In the transition to full electronic ignition, some systems used a combination of mechanical and electronic, with points controlling timing, and electronic systems to produce the spark. Most systems are now fully electronic, only the ignition timing being adjustable. On manual-start outboards the ignition system is fully autonomous, i.e. self-generating; on some electric-start engines use a battery-powered electronic ignition system with the obvious disadvantage that a discharged or damaged battery will prevent you from being able to start the engine by hand.

The reliability of these high-energy electronic ignition systems stems from their ability to produce a spark so powerful that even a heavily-fouled

spark plug will still fire. This has exorcised once and for all the old ghost
of unreliability that haunted two-stroke outboards in the past.

Engine management systems

A recent development in the outboard industry is the introduction of
computerised microprocessor-controlled engine management systems, of
which electronic ignition is just a part. Not only incorporating a monitoring
sub-system to warn when things are going wrong, it constantly adjusts the
ignition system and carburettors to make sure that everything is right. The
management system in addition monitors important engine functions such
as engine speed, crank angle, throttle position, and engine temperature.
Using these input parameters, ignition timing is adjusted by the micropro-
cessor so as to deliver optimum power. Settings can be further adjusted
to give a fast warm-up and prevent stalling.

Fuel systems

Small outboards with integral fuel tanks rely on gravity feed to transfer
fuel through the filter to the carburettor. This naturally puts physical
restrictions on the position and size of the tank, which is why some
manufacturers, despite the integral tank, still fit a fuel pump as standard
to their smaller outboards. This gives an additional benefit on some models,
in that the engine can draw from a separate tank as well as the integral
tank if necessary.

*Fig. 11. A good-sized fuel filter for the
job: transparent bowl to show when it's
dirty, and a reusable nylon filter
element.*

Outboard engines are fitted with at least one fuel filter, often more than one. Usually the fuel tank will have a gauze filter around the fuel pickup (or drain, if the tank is a gravity-fed integral type). A paper element or nylon filter fitted in-line before the fuel pump doubles as a sediment bowl/water separator on larger outboards, and another gauze filter actually at the fuel pump is usual.

To reduce the chances of vapour lock associated with the high temperatures that can build up under the cowling of an engine, some manufacturers use water-cooled fuel pumps. Some designs of smaller outboards have adopted a one-piece fuel pump and carburettor for compactness (Figure 12).

Larger engines require more fuel, and so are often fitted with two or more fuel pumps.

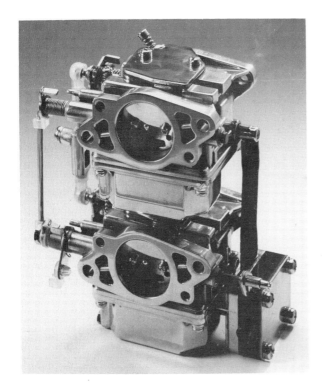

Fig. 12. Twin carburettors, the lower with integral fuel pump.

Developed initially for racing, several brands offer sports versions of their largest V6 engines with an electronic fuel injection (EFI) system replacing the standard carburettor model (Figure 13).

Carburettors come in a wide variety of shapes and sizes and normally have non-adjustable jets, the size of jet having been selected by the

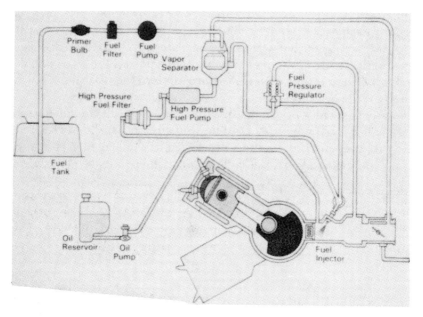

Fig. 13. The Suzuki fuel injection system.

manufacturer after extensive testing. In some cases—for example, where the boat is used on a lake in the mountains—jet changes will be required, but this is very much a specialised job best left to the manufacturer or importer.

The throttle stop screw should not be mistaken for an idle speed adjustment. Unlike other engines, outboards usually rely on retarding the ignition timing to adjust the idle speed once the carburettor reaches its minimum opening position.

Starting

Outboards destined for pleasure use offer electric start either standard or as an option on models as low as 5hp. Above 20hp the availability of manual starts drops, and above 40hp they disappear altogether, i.e. only electric start is available. But even with electric-start models, you can always get an emergency start by winding a rope round the flywheel and pulling it, in the old-fashioned way.

It is perhaps worth pointing out that the electric start is more of a convenience than a necessity. Outboards with 1800cc V4 engines are sold with manual starters for commercial applications. The largest engine I have personally started on the flywheel with a rope was a 150hp six-cylinder outboard, which started with less effort than many a smaller twin-cylinder engine.

Manual starters, often called recoil or repeater starters, fall into two basic types, sheave and pinion. The sheave type has a large-diameter sheave or disc sitting on top of the flywheel. It gives a much better pull, and is generally less troublesome. The pinion type is more compact, and sits beside the engine, but it tends to turn the engine over more slowly than the sheave type, and seems to cause more trouble in use.

If the manual starter appears jammed, and won't pull, the chances are that the gearshift isn't in neutral. Outboards over 5hp usually have a safety interlock that prevents the engine from being started in gear: a manual starter is prevented from being pulled by a lock, whereas on an electric-start engine a switch breaks a circuit.

A word of caution. When trying to remove a manual starter of the sheave type, never be tempted to undo the screw or nut located in the centre of the cowl. This will release the main spring, and you will probably have to take the engine to a workshop to have the spring replaced.

Bracket

The bracket holds the outboard to the boat, and is fixed on the transom by clamp screws and/or bolts. Very small outboards, about 2hp, may have only one clamp screw. This is really minimal: more usual is two screws,

Fig. 14. An outboard auxiliary bracket.

which will be enough up to the point where the outboard can no longer be considered portable—i.e. 25–40hp, depending on the brand.

A useful feature of many screw-clamp brackets is that you can pass the staple of a padlock through the screw handles as a disincentive to the thief. Upwards of 5hp, the bracket will be pre-drilled for transom bolts: this is always to be recommended, and essential with all outboards of 20hp and above. In fact, this is why larger outboards have dispensed with clamp screws, to force the bracket to be bolted.

One difficulty which sometimes arises when clamping the outboard to a transom is that the transom may be too thick or too thin. The former may occur if a small outboard is to be used as an auxiliary or reserve motor on a transom built for a large, high-power outboard. Under these circumstances trimming the transom is a rather drastic measure, so a better solution would be to use a separate auxiliary motor bracket for the small outboard (Figure 14).

If the transom is too thin, it may not be strong enough for the outboard you want to mount there. If that is not the case—for example, because it is made of steel plate—the transom can be thickened with a piece of wood. Special care, though, should be taken to bolt or otherwise secure the outboard to the boat, as the extra piece of wood may slip, and the outboard disappear over the side.

Brackets of portable outboards usually have some ring or eyelet to which you can attach a safety rope or chain, the other end of the chain being made fast to a strongpoint on the boat. Using this facility could prevent you losing your outboard. Watching your outboard disappearing into the depths produces a similar sensation to dropping your wallet full of cash overboard! Take my advice—always use a safety rope.

Two systems are used to attach the outboard to the bracket so that it can swivel and therefore steer the boat. The smallest outboards have no reverse shift; instead, they can be rotated through 360°. This allows you to get reverse thrust by swivelling the whole motor through 180° until it points in the opposite direction.

The 360° design, however, entails compromises, and if the model has a full gearshift, a different method of attachment is used. Saddle suspension, as it is called, is much stronger, holds the outboard more rigidly, and can incorporate features like power trim, remote control steering, even power steering. It also transmits less vibration to the boat.

One of the advantages of an outboard over the inboard, as we have said, is that its suspension is designed to tilt the whole engine up instantly if the leg strikes an underwater object or runs aground. In normal (forward) driving, with both 360° and saddle suspension types the lower unit is free to tilt; but if you select reverse you have to engage a reverse lock to prevent the outboard tilting up and leaving the propeller running in air. In many small outboards and all larger models this lock operates automatically, which makes life rather simpler.

A certain standardisation in the boat industry has led to boatbuilders using approximately the same angle for their transoms, but inevitably there will be some boat designs where the angle differs considerably from the norm. To allow for different transom angles the position of the outboard can be moved in or out by altering the position of the tilt pin (Figure 15).

Fig. 15. An outboard clamp bracket.

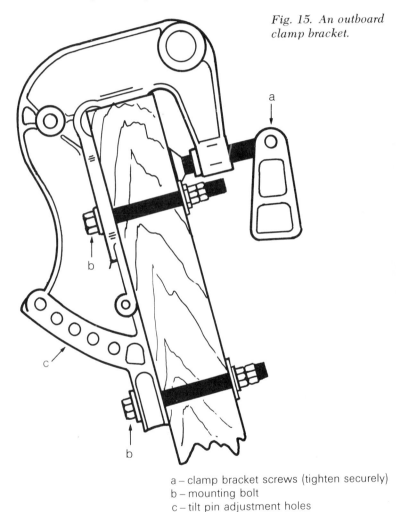

a – clamp bracket screws (tighten securely)
b – mounting bolt
c – tilt pin adjustment holes

Not to be confused with the function of the tilt pin, the shallow water drive feature offered on most outboards is a simple way of tilting up and holding the outboard at an angle so that the propeller and therefore the lower unit aren't so deep in the water. As its name suggests, it is used when negotiating shallow water and should only be operated with partial throttle.

After tilting the outboard it can be held in the up position using the tilt lock if provided. On no account should the tilt lock be used to keep the outboard up during trailering, because if the lock either breaks or unlocks itself the lower unit and propeller could be smashed.

Most portable outboards offer a carrying handle or hand grip, often incorporated in the bracket. There are some points to look out for here. First, and most important, is the handle suitable? In my experience of testing most of the different brands of outboard, many leave a lot to be desired in this respect. Is the handle large enough to get your hand round it without skinning your knuckles? It is one thing lifting up the outboard in a showroom, when your fingers are warm and the handle clean and dry, but something else when your cold, wet hands are gripping an oily handle as you negotiate a slippery jetty!

All outboards with the exception of the smallest 2hp models are offered with short or long shafts. The problem, however, is that the carrying handle is likely to be in the same position for both versions. This compromise usually means, depending on the skill of the manufacturer, that if the handle is well balanced with a short-shaft engine, the lower unit will be bumping along the ground with the long version. Or worse, if the handle has been designed for the long-shaft model, the package will be top-heavy in its short-shaft version, and the propeller will ride higher than the engine. Gravity will then ensure that any water remaining in the water pump, exhaust and lower unit will run back into the cylinders. The engine must be kept higher than the propeller at all times.

Lower unit

The main purpose of the lower unit is to transfer the rotation of the vertical drive shaft from the engine to the horizontal propeller shaft. But the same casing houses components to fulfil a number of other functions: the water inlet and water pump; the clutch, reduction gearbox and, where fitted, forward-neutral-reverse gearshift; the propeller and its shaft; a trim tab, a sacrificial anode (sometimes both functions are combined in one unit); and the underwater exhaust outlet.

Earlier lower unit designs had a casing split horizontally into two parts which were bolted together. Generally today's outboards have a one-piece housing which is less likely to leak and stronger, and can therefore be made lighter. Machining the complex shape of the one-piece housing used to be a long and expensive operation requiring several different processes. Since the introduction of computer-controlled machine tools, the whole casing can be finished at one go, which is why the one-piece housing is universal for all but a few models.

The reduction gearbox operates on a fixed ratio which is set by the manufacturer and cannot be changed. It usually contains a forward gear, reverse gear, and dog clutch, although some small engines and special racing models have no clutch and/or no reverse. It is important to realise that a dog clutch is not like the clutch of a car, which can be 'slipped': instead, it is either engaged or not engaged, connecting or disconnecting the propeller to/from the drive shaft. A dog clutch has no intermediate position and any attempt to 'slip' it—i.e. to engage gear slowly and progressively—will cause rapid damage, leading to premature gearbox failure. The clutch must therefore be engaged quickly and positively with a firm decisive movement.

On twin-engine installations, better handling is obtained by using outboards whose propellers rotate in opposite directions. This is known as contra-rotation. Most of the larger outboards (135hp and upwards) offer contra-rotating models; some achieve this by designing the engine so that the crankshaft rotates in the opposite direction, others by altering the gearbox so that only the propeller shaft contra-rotates, but in each case the lower unit has been designed specifically for the job. Some enthusiasts have tried to achieve contra-rotation by running one outboard all the time shifted in reverse, fitted with an opposite-rotation propeller. Unfortunately, outboard gearboxes are designed to run in reverse only at part throttle and only for short periods for manoeuvring etc. If run in reverse at high throttle settings they will break up within a matter of hours.

Exhaust gases emerge from the outboard either under the anti-ventilation plate (AVP)—sometimes, incorrectly, called the cavitation plate or anti-cavitation plate—or through the hub of the propeller. The former system has the advantage that both lower unit and propeller are less complicated and therefore cheaper to make, but can result in a noisier engine. If the outboard isn't mounted low enough, an air pocket can develop, letting exhausts and all the noise discharge above the water surface, to the discomfort of other water users.

The through-hub exhaust system, sometimes called Jet Prop, does bury the exhaust effectively underwater, but is more expensive to manufacture. It follows therefore that it tends to be used on larger outboards, above 5hp.

Special 'sail' versions of outboards for sailing yachts and other heavy, non-planing boats have an unusual lower unit design which is big enough to carry gears with a larger reduction ratio and swing a larger-diameter propeller. Some designs incorporate a double anti-ventilation plate to stop exhaust gases being sucked into the propeller when reversing. If this is allowed to happen, the propeller blades will lose their grip on the water and thrust will suffer.

Straight-cut gear teeth are simpler to make and are widely used on small outboards. As powers increase the teeth tend to whine, which is why the

*Fig. 16. Straight (right)
and spiral-cut (left) bevel
gears.*

larger models move over to spiral gears (Figure 16). The gears themselves
are adjusted in the gear housing using shims to ensure that their position
with respect to one another is exactly correct. No gear housing is identical,
so during assembly the number of shims required for the individual
housing is measured with very accurate equipment. If the shims are wrong,
or get lost during rebuilding of the lower unit, rapid gear wear and
premature breakage will occur.

Shaft lengths

Some years ago now the outboard industry standardised shaft lengths to
give boatbuilders unified transom heights (Figure 17) to which they should
build their boats. The most common lengths are given in Figure 18.

Most of the smallest outboards are only offered in short-shaft versions,
reflecting the size of boat they are destined for. Short-shaft outboards are

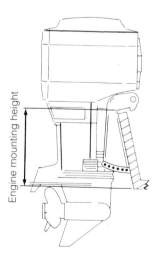

Fig. 17. Transom (engine mounting) height.

Engine mounting height

Usual designation	Common abbreviation	Nominal transom height	
		inch	mm
short	S	15	380
long	L	20	508
ultra/extra long	UL/EL/XL	25	635
super ultra long	SUL	27.5	700
extra extra long	XXL	30	762

Fig. 18. Table of transom heights and shaft lengths.

usual on small dinghies and inflatables, but moving up to rowing boats, runabouts etc, the standard is the long-shaft. In the last decade, as outboard powers have topped 200hp, making them suitable for larger boats, the extra long shaft has gained popularity and is widely used on seagoing craft such as sports fishing boats and especially on US boats.

European boatbuilders have adopted the extra long shaft rather slowly, mainly because seagoing boats with this level of power requirement would normally be fitted with an inboard or sterndrive. The trend has been for new outboards over 240hp to be available only with extra long or extra extra long shafts, forcing the boatbuilders to increase the transom heights (and consequently the freeboard) of these large boats: from the point of view of safety, a welcome trend.

The majority of the 'sail' model derivatives also use unusually long shaft lengths, but for a different reason. On a slow-moving boat, if the propeller is too near the surface, there is a chance of it sucking in air, causing loss of thrust because the propeller is turning in air instead of water. Also, on a boat with a relatively long waterline, if the shaft is too short the prop may lift out of the water as the boat pitches in waves. This may also occur in calm waters if too much weight is transferred to the bows, such as when two or three of the crew go forward to raise the anchor. For these reasons, the 'sail' outboards usually have L, XL, or even SUL shafts.

You need to be very careful that the shaft length is correct for the type of boat. While it is advantageous to have an unusually long shaft on a slow-moving or displacement boat, it is highly undesirable on a fast or planing boat. At speed, the over-long shaft will protrude into the water behind the boat and the energy required to drag the lower unit and shaft through the water will greatly slow the boat down—in fact it may not even be able to get up on the plane. In effect, it will act as a small sea anchor, which is the very last thing you want on a planing boat!

Always check before buying an outboard that its shaft length is appropriate for the boat. Changing the shaft length is impractical: the only solution is to replace the outboard with one of the correct shaft length.

If you buy certain types of speedometer, you may find that the sensor has to be fitted to the boat's stern. Most of today's outboards above the portable size have a speedometer pick-up sensor already in the lower unit, to ease its installation, so if you intend to fit a speedo it may be worth looking out for this feature.

Depending on the direction of propeller rotation there is a tendency for the prop to push the boat more to one side than the other when driving at speed (to port with the usual right-hand rotation propeller). To counteract this tendency, and balance the steering, a trim tab is positioned on the AVP just behind the propeller. It is unpainted because it is a sacrificial anode to protect the outboard from corrosion. Adjustment is covered in Chapter 4.

Cooling water is drawn into the pump through inlet holes in the lower unit: depending on the engine model, they are covered with a sieve strainer to prevent weed or other foreign objects from being sucked into the cooling system. From time to time the inlet holes should be checked for blockage.

No matter how good the oil seals are in a lower unit, water always manages to enter. It emulsifies the oil during running, and rarely causes any problems provided the oil is changed according to the manufacturer's instructions. Unfortunately if the gear oil is replenished at the start of the new season, rather than at the end of the old season, and the outboard is left over winter in freezing temperatures, any water in the lower unit will freeze, producing such expansive forces that the housing can be split open, or otherwise irreparably damaged. Changing the gear oil in the lower unit is covered later in Chapter 5.

2   *Choosing the right engine*

GENERAL POINTS

Buying an outboard requires a good deal of thought—about your own requirements as well as what the manufacturers have on offer. Although specifications vary from brand to brand, there are certain features which tend to be common to all engines of that size. It is worth going through these briefly before going on to discuss the more individual features.

The smallest outboards made by each manufacturer, about 2hp, have built-in fuel tanks, and neither gearshift nor clutch. The slightly larger 3hp models offer a clutch, but for most brands it is necessary to move up to at least 4hp for a full FNR (forward, neutral and reverse) gearshift, as well as the option of a separate fuel tank. Lighting coils to run navigation lights or charge a battery are a valuable plus, and are offered on most outboards from about 6hp upwards.

Outboards of up to about 5hp can be considered portable, although an engine much over 3hp is already too heavy for most ladies and children. Depending on the brand, 20–25hp is the upper limit of what might be called transportables or 'luggables', not only because of their weight and size, but also because anything larger tends to be fitted with electric start and remote control; larger engines therefore require installation, where for the smaller models fitting is simply a matter of bolting them on to the transom and plugging in the fuel line.

Some manufacturers sell a manual-start 40hp outboard with tiller for semi-commercial applications, but an outboard of this size is approaching the limit for two persons to carry.

Remote control starts as low as 5hp, 6hp with electric start, but is more usual on outboards from 20hp upwards. It becomes essential at 25–30hp, depending on the brand. Starting at a similar engine size is automatic oil mixing as standard, although some manufacturers offer it either standard or as an accessory right down to 2.5hp.

Power trim, which can be considered as a performance enhancer, is offered on most brands as an accessory from 40hp, and is usually standard over 100hp. Larger boats using twin outboards can benefit from contra-rotating propellers, available on engines over 120hp. Some models over

200hp offer the luxury of power steering. This information is given in tabular form in Appendix D, Figure 54.

WHICH BOAT?

When buying an outboard, your choice of engine will be very much predetermined by the type of boat you have. It is outside the scope of an outboard manual to cover boat selection in detail, but a few brief remarks may be worthwhile to readers who have not yet bought a boat.

The answers to the questions how, who, where and when will define the options available. **How** is the boat to be used? Is it to be trailered, or kept in a marina? Or will it be carried on a roof rack, or kept on board a larger boat or yacht? Often the car size/power will determine a weight/size limitation on the boat. Do you want to be fastest round the bay, or just want to potter up and down the river? Do you want to go water skiing, or go sea angling?

Next, **who** will be using the boat: a couple? Mum, Dad and the children? Mainly the children? If the latter, how old are they? How many people will be on board at one time? **Where** will the boat be used? Will it be at a nearby marina, or hundreds of miles away; on a sheltered inland lake or on the open sea? Will it be used in a different place each time, or always in the same place? Also, where do you live? Have you a secure place to store the boat in winter, in your garden or driveway, or do you live in an apartment?

When is the boat to be used? How often, and also what time of year? From April through to October, or just during the summer months? Will it be used every week through the season, or for a few weeks only during the annual holiday?

The answers to these questions should narrow down the choice of boat. For example, if the boat will be used once a year during the summer holidays, hundreds of miles from your city apartment, maybe you should be considering an inflatable boat: no permanent mooring charges, no trailer to tow around on holiday, no extra ferry charges, and no trailer parking problems for the rest of the year.

If you haven't yet chosen a boat, make a note of your answers under the who, what, where, and when headings and take it along with you to your boat dealer. Having done your homework, the choice of boat will not be difficult.

Inflatable dinghies

As this type of craft is nigh impossible to row efficiently, an outboard is a necessity rather than a luxury. First point to look out for: if there is no transom, there **must** be a bracket on which to mount the outboard. Check the boatbuilder's plate/label for the maximum recommended outboard power. All small dinghies take outboards with a short shaft. Unless you expect to make trips much longer than an hour in the boat, an outboard with a built-in tank will be adequate, and will save room—though it's a good idea always to carry a spare can of fuel to top up if necessary. If you are often going alongside, as you would with a tender, a neutral/clutch is useful so you don't keep having to shut off and restart the engine. Look for an outboard that is light and has a good carrying handle.

Fig. 19. Inflatable with outboard.

Rigid dinghies

Modern glassfibre and aluminium dinghies often have short transoms, the more traditional designs in glassfibre or wood tending to favour long transoms, which allow the greater freeboard (higher sides) desirable in waves. Heavier than their inflatable counterparts, they require higher engine powers, and the increased fuel consumption makes it preferable to use a separate fuel tank. The tank usually can be stowed under a seat, so there is no loss of space, and if the boat is a lightweight one, positioning the tank in the bows can improve the hull trim (balance) when you are on your own and controlling the engine from the stern.

Sports inflatables & RIBs (rigid hull inflatables)

To be able to enjoy boating during the annual holidays, and then be able to deflate the boat, carry it in or on top of a compact car, and store it in the attic, cellar or garage until next year has brought water sports to a large group of people who otherwise would not have been able to enjoy boating. The sports inflatable is a sophisticated version of the inflatable dinghy that shares the dinghy's stowability and yet has features such as inflatable keels, vee-hulls and rigid floors that give it the performance potential of a rigid sportsboat.

As this type of boat lies on the border between a fixed installation and a (trans)portable one which is set up for a holiday, then dismantled afterwards, it is important at the outset to decide which side of the fence you want to sit on! If you want true portability, you will have to compromise on engine power, going for an engine size of up to 25hp for family use, with a maximum of 40hp for group (e.g. diving club) use. Water skiing will be compromised, and limited if under 40hp: the lower limit for skiing is 40hp, although lightweight skiers may make do with a 25hp outboard, and children one of 8hp! Mariner, Mercury and Yamaha produce special accessories to use their 40hp models on inflatables: an extra carrying handle, and a special bracket to aid clamping the engine to the transom.

RIBs, with their rigid glassfibre hull and inflatable tubes, offer admirable sea keeping characteristics, which is one of the main reasons for their popularity as rescue launches and lifeboats. The moulded interior of the RIB's glassfibre hull is easier to clean than a pure inflatable's, where sand etc. quickly disappears into the space between the floor and the boat's bottom.

Fig. 20. RIB with outboard.

The weight advantage of the inflatable and its compact size when deflated is less applicable to the RIB. Any RIB larger than a dinghy really has to be transported on a trailer, which removes one of the main advantages of the inflatable—not having to trailer.

With both RIBs and sports inflatables, look out for the transom height: some take short-shaft engines, some long-shaft. If you intend to use remote control, check how the steering and throttle/shift control box will be mounted: some designs are very impractical to use. An electric-start outboard, for all its convenience, may be something of a disadvantage in an inflatable. There is the weight and size of the battery, which must be very securely tied down, otherwise it can break loose and spill acid over the fabric. Then there are the extra cables, and an ignition key to get lost in the sand!

The fuel tank too must be securely attached. Better still, right from the start, buy a flexible fuel tank. They don't bump into your leg when carried, they don't rust, they don't scratch the floor or tubes of the boat, and they take the form of the bows, or the inside of a locker. At the end of the holiday you just roll the tank up and stow it in a locker or even a drawer.

Engines of 50hp and upward to 85hp mounted on an inflatable give a very potent combination of speed and safety, which effectively brings this group into the next class, that of runabouts and ski boats.

Runabouts and ski boats

To give a reasonable top speed, and allow water skiing, you should be looking at outboards with a minimum of 40hp. Most of the features found on large outboards extend down to the 40s, which means that you can create a fulfilling outboard/boat combination, limited only by the size of your budget. Full instrumentation, automatic oil mixing, electric start all

Fig. 21. Outboard-powered runabout.

add up to create a boat that is complete in every way. Power trim, if available, is another feature well worth the extra expenditure.

Almost all runabouts manufactured today take a long-shaft outboard, but it is still wise to check. The outboard comes complete with remote control box, and in most cases the dealer will provide the cables and propeller. Some models, especially those with electric start, offer a tachometer as standard.

Boats for uncompromised water skiing need a minimum of 80hp, and much more for slalom, barefoot and trick skiing—200hp is essential for competition.

The American bass boat

This specialised type of boat developed for bass fishing enjoys tremendous popularity in the United States. The hull bottom is relatively flat as they are only used on inland lakes for freshwater rod fishing. Special propellers giving quick acceleration on powerful outboards of 150–200hp are set high in the water for a fast top speed, so that the angler can get to the rich fishing areas first. Once there, the main outboard is stopped and tilted up, and a small electric outboard is then used to propel the craft closer inshore to where the fish are.

Electronic sonar fish finders help to locate the best places to fish. The boats are equipped with built-in bait and fish tanks, complete with water recirculator. As the end of the competition nears, the main outboard powers the boat back to base at full throttle, just in time for the weigh-in. With prize payouts exceeding $100,000 it is easy to understand the continuing growth of this type of boating.

Fig. 22. American bass boat with electric outboard in the bow.

Small cruisers 15–20ft

In this group, we are talking about fast planing hulls rather than slow river cruisers, which are dealt with below. An outboard of at least 60hp would give a small cruiser enough power to plane comfortably, with something in reserve for extra loads or occasional water skiing, and to compensate for a 'dirty bottom' caused by weed growth. As boat lengths increase, so must the engine power, so that a 20ft cruiser would require in the region of 115hp. Power trim is recommended, and automatic oil mixing. If there are many electrical appliances on board, compare alternator specifications when choosing an outboard. Usual for these sizes of motor is an alternator output of about 80W: options giving as much as 180W are on offer depending on the brand.

Fig. 23. Small day cruiser with outboard.

River and canal cruisers

This grouping applies to slow, displacement-hull boats for inland waters. The lower boat speeds mean that high power is unnecessary—in fact, unwelcome. All that is required of the engine is to be able to push the boat up to its maximum hull speed, plus a little more as a reserve in case of strong winds, currents etc. The maximum theoretical speed of a displacement hull can be calculated from the formula:

speed (kts) = $1.34 \times \sqrt{\text{waterline length (ft)}}$

Four-stroke outboards, such as Honda's or Yamaha's, are very popular for this type of use because their extra size and weight over two-stroke engines is of little consequence. The outboards are usually a permanent fixture on the boat, so portability and weight do not enter the argument. The advantages of the four-cycle outboard—smoother, quieter running, absence of smoking at idle, and lower fuel consumption—do.

Claims are sometimes made that the four-stroke engine is cleaner than the two-stroke because it has no oil escaping into the water through the exhaust. The argument appears to be more political than scientific. The modern two-stroke outboard operates on a fuel-oil ratio of at least 50:1, as low as 150:1 with automatic lubrication systems, and also burns more efficiently than its predecessors: this, and the fact that it now uses biodegradable oils, keeps its potential for damaging the environment to a minimum.

Fig. 24. Outboard-powered river cruiser.

Displacement hulls take time to stop once they get going: using a standard outboard to try to stop a moving displacement boat is not that straightforward. What happens is that in reverse, exhaust gases become sucked into the propeller, and the propeller actually turns in air, rather than in water. The result is that reverse thrust is low, and the boat takes a long time to stop—a very important point in inland cruising.

Most outboard manufacturers have overcome this problem by using a special propeller or lower unit, usually designated 'sail model' or something similar. If you own an existing outboard, and want to improve its performance in this respect, you will have to fit a special propeller or modification such as the Finze Thrust Booster (address in Appendix E).

The size of outboard required to reach the hull's theoretical maximum speed will be recommended by the boatbuilder. It is, however, worthwhile buying a larger outboard than specified so that a good speed can be maintained with the motor running at partial (half or two-thirds) throttle. Good seamanship requires keeping something in reserve, and it is always good to know that there is some extra power there for emergencies such as exceptionally strong headwinds, currents, or even towing another boat.

Also, it is much more pleasant to listen to a larger outboard running at half-throttle all day than a small one at full speed—and there will most likely be a fuel saving with the larger engine as well!

Although power requirements are low on inland waters, it is worth moving one step up from the basic engine. Full remote control with electric start saves your having to lean over the stern of the boat every time it has to be started. For this, a lighting coil with rectifier will be needed, in order to charge the battery.

A popular size of engine for inland waterways is 9.9hp. Depending on the brand, many 9.9s are detuned 15s, so as long as it doesn't overpower the boat, it may be worth paying the extra to get the full 15hp. The 6hp and 8hp are also often different versions of the same model, which is, incidentally, the largest model to use half-sized fuel tanks: above 8hp, most outboard manufacturers use the full-size 24-litre (5 Imp gallons) tank.

Sailboat auxiliaries and back-up engines

The outboard attributes of low installation cost and ease of removal when not in use make it a popular choice as an auxiliary on sailing yachts up to about 25ft, beyond which the inboard takes over.

Because of the special requirements of this application, most manufacturers produce a special 'sail' model specifically for this purpose. Its transom height is much longer, so that the propeller doesn't come out of the water in waves, or when the crew are standing in the bows. An arrangement is made to keep the exhaust gases in reverse clear of the propeller. The starter rope guide is changed so that it can be pulled vertically rather than horizontally. Extensions to the throttle and shift controls can be fitted to allow their operation from the cockpit.

As a general rule, a 20ft boat would require an 8hp outboard, while a 25-footer would need 15hp. Smaller day boats under 16ft would be adequately powered by an outboard of 5hp, although if the motor is only used when becalmed, a 3hp would be quite sufficient.

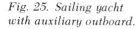

Fig. 25. Sailing yacht with auxiliary outboard.

Depending on the waters to be cruised, and the time of day, an outboard with a lighting coil for navigation lights may be a necessity. So check with your dealer to see if it is available standard or as an accessory.

Some yachts are supplied with a built-in outboard mounting, often in a 'well' behind the cockpit. If not, there are several models of auxiliary motor bracket on the market made specially for this purpose, some fixed and some retractable so that the outboard can be lifted clear of the water when sailing. Retractables are usually spring-loaded to counteract the weight of the outboard: to lower the engine you simply push it down until a clip engages, to raise it you disengage the clip and lift. Some of the more elaborate brackets not only retract the engine, but allow it to swivel through 90° so that it doesn't stick out at the stern when not in use.

These brackets are also used on motor boats where a low-power outboard is used as a back-up or emergency motor in case the main engine fails. Sterndrive users can attach a tie bar accessory to the outboard so that the main engine steering wheel also steers the outboard. If the main engine uses petrol, it is logical to have a four-stroke as back-up, so that they both can use the same fuel without the need to pre-mix a separate supply of two-stroke fuel. Using an outboard with automatic oil mixing is another way of eliminating the necessity of using premix.

Engine sizes for back-up power are usually in the region of 8–15hp, but this figure varies widely according to boat size and personal preference.

Racing boats

We don't have room here to cover all the different outboard classes raced in all the motor boating countries in the world: the choice is between circuit racing, which takes place on inland waters and is uniquely out-board-powered, and offshore, where competitors are not confined to out-boards but may fit any engine that meets the class limits. In the top classes this can produce monstrous rigs powered by as many as six outboard engines. For the enthusiasts, the main international circuit racing classes for 1992 are listed below.

Formula 1: homologated (special racing) catamarans 2000cc.

Formula 3: O: 850, homologated (special racing) 751–850cc catamarans.

Formula 4: S: 850, catamarans with stock (standard) 751–850cc outboards.

Formula 5: catamarans with stock (standard) outboards 551–750cc.

There is a multitude of other outboard classes, starting as low as 10hp for children.

The catamarans and monohulls used for racing are specially built for that purpose. If you want to go deeper into this subject, contact your national powerboat racing federation—in the UK the sport is admini-stered by the RYA—or the world racing body, the UIM (addresses in Appendix E).

Offshore sports fishing boats

Sports fishing or sea angling requires a solid boat with good sea keeping qualities. Because the boat will be used offshore, with the risk of being caught in bad weather, a twin-outboard installation is recommended for reliability. Particular attention should be paid, when choosing the engines, to how effective the cowling is at keeping water out of the hood. Some cowls are not as waterproof as they appear, and will allow water to enter when large waves sweep the stern.

Boats with higher transom heights than usual provide greater freeboard, and a greater margin of safety. It is therefore preferable for sea angling boats to be built for extra long shaft (25in/635mm) outboards. The out-board needs to generate a generous supply of electricity to run all the electrical equipment, including bilge pump, fish tank/bait pumps, echo sounder, fishfinder, radio, radar etc., and you can buy models with alter-nators that will deliver up to 35A per engine. Engine power recommenda-tions depend very much on the hull shape and loads to be carried; your best source of advice will be the boatbuilder.

SINGLE OR TWIN?

From time to time boating magazines publish comparison tests of the same boat, one with twin engines, the other with a single. To obtain similar performance the twin engines have to add up to approximately

40% more power than the single: for example, to produce the same speed as a 100hp single outboard, you would need to fit twin 70hp units. This brings us on to the main disadvantage of the twin-engine configuration, which is its cost. Not only will two 70s cost more than one 100, but you also have to add in an extra set of controls, two batteries, steering arrangement for two engines, possibly extra instrumentation. Running costs would be higher, the twin's extra weight and drag increasing its fuel consumption. On economics, therefore, the single engine wins hands down.

But cost is not the only criterion: good seamanship is even more important. Depending on the replies to the how, who, when, and where questions we asked at the beginning of the chapter, the twin-engine configuration is still the better choice for most offshore boating because of its reliability and safety.

3   Setting up

FITTING YOUR OUTBOARD

Single-engine installation

Single-engine installations should normally be mounted on a vertical line through the centre of the stern. On displacement boats, this may not be practical: the ideal position may already be occupied by the rudder, for instance, or on a sailing hull the sweeping counter may make it necessary to mount the outboard on the side of the boat. Fortunately the position of the outboard is not critical on a displacement hull, where the offset thrust of the propeller can be compensated by steering the outboard a little to one side. More often the steering of the outboard is clamped at the correct angle, and the boat's rudder is used to steer.

On planing hulls, with few exceptions, the outboard must be mounted in the centre of the transom. The first task is therefore to find and mark off the transom centreline. The larger the boat, the greater the importance to get this line exactly right: remember, the outboard will be attached with bolts, and we don't want to end up drilling so many holes in the transom that it ends up like a Gruyère cheese!

One of the simplest and most accurate ways to determine the centreline is with a pencil and a piece of string. This is similar to the procedure we learned at school for bisecting a line using compasses. Make a loop in the string so that it is just longer than half the width of the transom. Hold

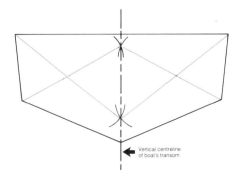

Vertical centreline
of boat's transom

Fig. 26. Finding the transom centreline.

the end of the string at the top left corner of the transom where it meets the deck, and with the pencil fixed in the loop, draw an arc on the transom.

Now, without changing the length of the string, move the end to the top right corner of the transom, and draw another arc. The two arcs will intersect on the centreline of the transom. Draw at least two more pairs of arcs from different positions on either side of the transom (including the point where the vee-bottom meets the side of the hull) and draw a line through the intersections. This will be the exact centreline.

At the beginning of the chapter we said that the outboard is normally mounted on the transom centreline. One exception would be a rig consisting of a high-powered outboard installed on a light boat, such as a 115hp 16-foot sportsboat. In such cases handling will be improved by mounting the outboard 1–1½in to the right of the centreline (assuming that the propeller is a conventional right-handed one, rotating clockwise when going ahead). This offset counteracts the torque (turning action) of the propeller, which otherwise would give the boat a list at full throttle.

If in doubt, ask your dealer/boatbuilder. The experts will have done extensive tests and will best be able to advise you whether an offset is necessary, and if so how much it should be.

Mount the outboard on the transom centreline, offset if required. Clamp it in position using its own clamp screws, or as a temporary measure a carpenter's clamp.

The height at which the outboard motor is installed will influence the behaviour of the boat more than any other single item. Together with propeller selection it is the most common source of user dissatisfaction, because it can turn the best outboard in the world into a lemon!

On planing sportsboats, an outboard set too low in the water will cause unnecessary drag, slowing the boat down and wasting fuel. If it is too high, the propeller will ventilate (i.e. suck air from the surface), initially only in turns but eventually even on the straight. The ideal height for the engine is as high as it will go without ventilating.

On a series production boat, the boatbuilder will normally have determined the best height for the boat/outboard combination during a series of sea trials. Should this information not be available, the dealer will normally carry out the installation for you. But you may want to determine the correct height of the outboard motor yourself, in which case the procedure is described below.

As a starting point, the height of the outboard should be adjusted so as to bring the AVP (anti-ventilation plate, sometimes called the anti-cavitation plate) to the same height as the bottom of the boat. First, the trim angle should be adjusted so that the AVP is parallel to the boat's bottom. Use a straight piece of wood held along the boat's bottom to line up the outboard's AVP.

Fig 27. Motor mounting heights.

(a)
*Work application
(heavily loaded—slow
speed)*

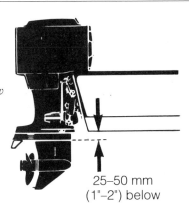

25–50 mm
(1"–2") below

(b)
*Normal duty
(average speed
installation)*

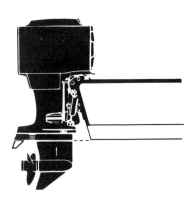

(c)
*Sport application
(sport and ski)*

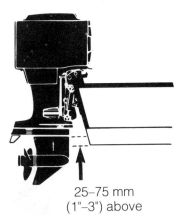

25–75 mm
(1"–3") above

If the AVP is more than 2in below the hull bottom, the outboard must be raised, using pieces of wood under the clamp bracket as spacers: if the plate is more than 2.5in above the bottom, it will have to be lowered, which will involve cutting a piece out of the transom. Before taking such a drastic step, however, it would be wise to discuss the proposed action with your dealer or boatbuilder.

Clamp the outboard in this position, and if the engine is 20hp or over, bolt it to the transom using the bolts supplied. Drill two holes through the transom at the **top** of the slots or uppermost pair of holes located in the lower part of the clamp bracket (Figure 28). The reason for using the top of the slots or upper pair of holes is to allow the engine to be raised if this is found necessary after initial sea trials, without having to drill further holes in the transom.

Fig. 28. Drilling the holes at the top of the slots.

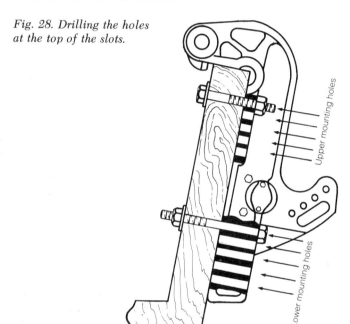

Make sure that you can drill a clear hole through on the inside of the transom before starting to drill. When inserting the transom bolts, it is important to seal around them with a marine sealant to prevent water leaking into the stern. This is doubly important if the transom is a wood/glassfibre sandwich, when the wood will soak up any water like blotting paper, leading to swelling and delamination and eventually ruining the transom.

Tighten the bolts securely, using the washers and locknuts supplied. Final adjustments to the height can only be made after the boat test.

For non-planing displacement boats, the object of the exercise will be the exact opposite. Here we are trying to position the propeller as deep as it will go, without risking the engine being swamped. This is the reason that outboards destined for displacement boats, e.g. sailing yachts, are fitted with a longer-than-usual shaft. They often have a larger or second anti-ventilation plate to reduce the possibility of the propeller sucking air.

Twin-engine installation

Every outboard manufacturer publishes a minimum separation figure for each model he produces. This dimension is the minimum clearance required in twin installations to prevent the engines touching each other when turning. If the separation plus the width of two engines exceeds the width of the transom, it may not be possible to fit a twin installation, although a boatbuilder may be able to modify the transom to the width required.

Because of the vee-bottom, a boat taking a single long-shaft outboard centrally mounted will need two short-shaft outboards in a twin installation. On larger boats, a single extra-long-shaft outboard is replaced by two long-shaft engines. This means that you are unlikely to be able to convert a single installation into a twin simply by buying and fitting another motor.

Boat handling can be improved with contra-rotating propellers, which are to be recommended if available. Having each propeller rotating in a different direction means that the torque on one exactly counteracts the torque on the other. Contra-rotation is usually achieved by using a standard powerhead and specially designed gear arrangement in the lower unit, but with some outboards the whole cycle is reversed—i.e. the crankshaft itself rotates in the opposite direction.

Not all outboards offer contra-rotation, so if you want it you will need to find out which models do before choosing your power units.

The two outboards are linked with a tie bar on the steering brackets, the steering cable (preferably a double cable to take the increased load) then being connected to just one of them. In other words, you steer one 'main' engine, usually the starboard one, and the second engine follows. Connecting the engines to separate cables will lead to heavy steering, and sooner or later jamming. This is especially the case if using power steering.

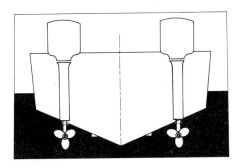

Fig. 29. Twin-engine installation: engines should be positioned directly behind spray rails.

As with the single installation, engine heights should be set so that the anti-ventilation plate is level with the base of the transom at the point where the outboard is fixed. If there are pronounced spray rails on the hull bottom, each engine should be positioned so as to be mounted directly behind one (see Figure 29).

Conventionally, engines with contra-rotating propellers are installed so as to make the propellers turn 'outward', i.e. the starboard propeller will turn clockwise, the port propeller counter-clockwise. The length of the tie bar should be adjusted so that the wakes of the outboards converge approximately 65–80ft astern of the boat, equivalent to an angle of about 3° toe-out. This 'preloads' the tie bar and the rest of the steering system: if the outboards are set up exactly parallel, play in the steering system will vibrate and give rise to 'chatter' (see Figure 30).

Fig. 30. Toeing-out twin outboards. The wakes should converge 65–80 ft (20–25 m) astern of the boat.

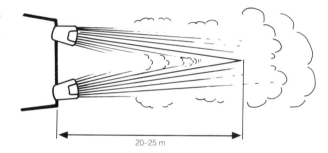

20–25 m

Performance brackets

The performance advantage gained by planing boats from concentrating the engine weight so far to the rear was explained in Chapter 1. An outboard is usually mounted on the transom, but it can be moved even further aft by using special brackets to hold the outboard off the stern.

These brackets resemble a cube-shaped box or space frame with sides of approximately 20in (500mm). The box is bolted to the transom, and the outboard is bolted to it, in effect moving the outboard 20in further aft.

Only considerable experience will tell you how best to position the outboard and bracket for maximum benefit; installation is therefore best done professionally. The principal use of these brackets is on high-performance rigs and racing boats. You need to take care when using them in rough seas that the outboard is not subjected to severe pounding by waves.

Installation in a motor well

The other type of installation requiring special attention is the 'well' type, often found in small sailing cruisers. Here the outboard sits in a well behind the cockpit, usually underneath a hatch for easy access.

There are two main considerations. Firstly, the outboard must have adequate ventilation. If the covering hatch seals the compartment tight, the engine cannot obtain air for combustion, and will just stop. The second requirement, often overlooked, is for a flexible pipe or tube to carry away exhaust from the exhaust relief holes.

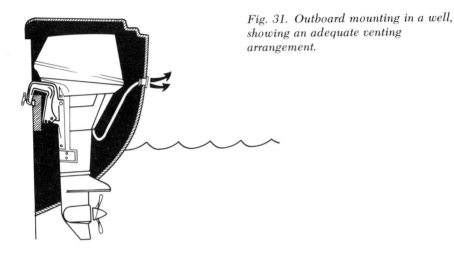

Fig. 31. Outboard mounting in a well, showing an adequate venting arrangement.

Exhaust gases normally exit down through the lower unit into the water, an arrangement that works perfectly when the boat is streaming through the water, and the throttle is partially open. At idle, however, the engine doesn't produce enough power to push the exhaust out underwater, so as a relief, small holes in the drive shaft housing allow the gases at low throttle to escape above the water surface into the atmosphere or into the well. Unless these relief gases are led away into the open, fumes will build up in the well and the outboard will suffocate in its own exhaust. Your local dealer will be able to supply you with a suitable system to lead the exhaust outside the well.

Engine trim

Power trim Power trim performs two distinct functions, trimming and tilting. The trim function moves the outboard in and out (i.e. towards or away from the stern) to change the angle the leg makes with the transom. Tilting is the lifting-up of the outboard to free a fouled propeller, or to prevent the lower unit from grounding or striking an underwater obstruction.

There is always a manual valve in the hydraulic circuit so that the outboard can be raised or lowered by hand in the event of the pump becoming inoperative. As often as not the culprit is not the power trim mechanism but a flat battery, and this manual valve will ensure the outboard can still be lowered into the water and started by rope.

Operation is simple. An electric motor drives a hydraulic pump that regulates the flow of oil to raise or lower the outboard, while a sensor shows the amount of trim angle on a gauge on the instrument panel. The trim switch is located on the throttle/gearshift, so that the driver does not have to take his hands off the throttle to change the trim. A shock absorber is usually incorporated into the power trim hydraulic cylinders to prevent any shocks experienced by the outboard being transmitted to the boat. Checking the level of hydraulic fluid from time to time is the only maintenance required.

Referred to earlier in the text as a 'performance enhancer', the power trim function allows the angle between the outboard and the boat to be finely adjusted to suit the boat speed. Watching an outboard race shows just how much power trim affects speed: if the power trim fails, it will not be very long before the unlucky boat is at the back of the pack!

First of all, initial acceleration is improved when the outboard is trimmed in, i.e. down. As the boat accelerates up to its maximum speed, further speed increases can only be achieved by reducing the amount of water in contact with the boat's hull. Power trim allows the driver while driving at speed to experiment with the dynamics of the boat to find the best balance between being trimmed in and trimmed out. Too far in, and there will be too much water in contact with the hull, increasing friction and reducing speed; too far out, and the prop will lose thrust or the boat become unstable. The most favourable position can, with practice, be 'felt' by the driver, and can be seen from the instruments (speedometer, tachometer and power trim indicator).

When driving at speed, as the trim is increased, the boat can come so far out of the water that there is no longer enough water to keep the boat up, so it will lean over to one side. The dynamic forces on the hull will try to correct this, pushing the boat over onto the other side, where the process will repeat itself. Failure to reduce trim or speed will keep the boat rolling (chine riding) from one side to the other with increasing amplitude. It could be compared to the swaying of a caravan that is going too fast. As in most things in life, if the warning signs are ignored, an accident is inevitable.

Always adjust the power trim gradually when driving fast. Although the trim tab (see later) is adjusted to give balanced steering at full throttle, changing the trim of the outboard will bring unbalanced forces to bear on the lower unit. Unless you have hydraulic steering, this will be immediately noticeable as heaviness on the steering wheel.

If the outboard is trimmed too far out the boat can start a cyclical pitching movement whereby the bows rise up, only to drop down again.

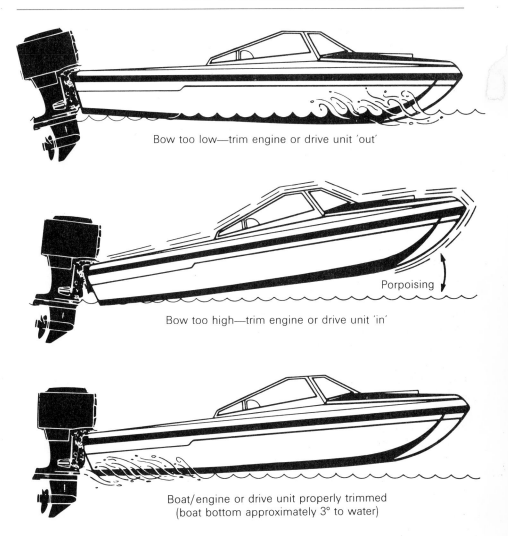

Bow too low—trim engine or drive unit 'out'

Porpoising

Bow too high—trim engine or drive unit 'in'

Boat/engine or drive unit properly trimmed
(boat bottom approximately 3° to water)

Fig. 32. Altering the trim of the outboard leg (the angle between engine and transom) to lift the bow higher or allow it to settle lower in the water.

This is another kind of instability, whereby the thrust from the propeller is trying to push the stern of the boat downward, and the bow up. The hull does its best to comply, but eventually the weight of the boat will be greater than the upwards force on the bow; at that point the bow will drop again, and the cycle will restart. This 'porpoising' gives an uncomfortable motion to the boat, and is quickly rectified by trimming the motor in. If porpoising cannot be eliminated by adjusting the trim angle, it may be due to a rocker hull bottom (see Chapter 6).

Driving over waves, there may be a tendency for the boat to develop a rhythmical pitching in time with the waves, similar to porpoising; here too, a more comfortable ride may be obtained by trimming the outboard in, which will reduce slamming.

Trim/tilt pin   Where the engine is not fitted with power trim, the trim angle can only be adjusted at rest, by altering the position of the tilt pin. There are normally 4–6 holes through which the pin can be positioned, to compensate for the different transom angles found on different boats. The standard transom angle is 13°, but this varies according to different boatbuilders, and may approach 0° (i.e. the transom is perpendicular to the boat's bottom) on some inflatables. The angle should be adjusted to bring the AVP parallel to the boat's bottom. Once the correct hole position is found, no further adjustment should be necessary.

Trim tab   On a single-engined boat, the rotation of the propeller causes the boat to move off the straight line into a gentle turn. This is corrected by turning the steering wheel slightly in the opposite direction. The amount of correction required at the steering wheel varies according to the boat speed, and the trim angle.

Larger outboards, usually above 15hp, are fitted with a combined sacrificial anode/trim tab which allows the steering to be balanced out at a particular speed and trim: normally at full throttle, and at the usual trim angle for that speed. Its correct position can only be found by boat testing and follows a simple rule. If the boat tends to veer off to port, i.e. to the left, move the trim tab to the left, and vice versa. To adjust it, a box or socket wrench is required to get at the securing bolt, which is sometimes covered by a removable plastic plug.

If correctly adjusted, the steering will be balanced under these conditions, and the boat should steer straight ahead if you let go of the wheel. Remember however, that as soon as the speed or trim angle is changed, the steering will no longer be balanced. This is particularly important with power trim, as the unbalancing forces can be quite strong, and can come on quickly for just a small change in trim angle.

Trim flaps/trim planes   A hull is designed to maintain the boat in a balanced state of trim, but if the boat has high sides or a large superstructure—as would be the case in a cabin cruiser—a strong side wind can heel it over slightly, unbalancing the hydrodynamic forces acting on the hull. Apart from being unpleasant, this enforced list makes for awkward boat handling: more steering correction is required to stay on course, and speed drops.

To compensate, trim flaps can be fitted to the transom. Operating individually, these can be used to push down on one side of the hull, thus

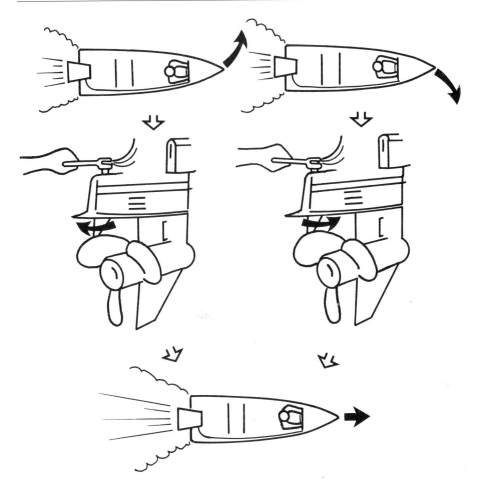

Fig. 33. Trim tab and its adjustment.

bringing the boat upright, back on trim. If no power trim is fitted, pushing both flaps down will bring the bows down, which may be desirable in rough sea conditions. If there is a permanent list even at rest, the source of the problem should be found and cured, rather than using the flaps just to treat the symptoms!

STEERING SYSTEMS

Rope and pulley

The cheapest steering system uses a rope wound round a drum behind the steering wheel, running astern to the outboard through pulley wheels mounted in each corner. Although cheap, this system has little else to commend it, and is unsuitable for anything but the smallest of outboards. It is far too easy for the rope to slip, or jump off the pulley, or tangle with some other piece of equipment, resulting in a total loss of steering control.

Cable systems

The standard steering arrangement for outboards is what is known as the Bowden cable or push-pull system. Here the rotary movement of the wheel is converted to linear movement in the steering box. The outer sleeve of the Bowden cable is fixed to the box, while the inner cable is inserted into the box in such a way that it slides in and out with every movement of the wheel.

At the outboard end the outer sleeve is fixed to the boat (or, in some cases, the engine), while the inner cable is connected to the outboard's steering arm. Care must be taken on installation to check that the steering is neither fouled nor damaged when the outboard is trimmed or tilted.

Double cable steering—where the cables are run round both sides of the boat so that one cable pulls while the other pushes—can be used on installations of 100hp and upwards, and certainly should be used if total engine power exceeds 200hp. Apart from the safety benefit, double cables reduce play, and result in more positive steering.

Hydraulic steering

In a single-engine installation, as power increases it becomes impossible to set up the engine/boat combination so as to give neutral steering under all conditions. This is especially true of engines with power trim. The steering can be set up for a particular throttle position and trim angle, so that the boat keeps a steady course without a hand at the wheel. But as soon as the throttle setting is altered, or the trim adjusted, the steering can become quite heavy.

It is important to differentiate between permanent heaviness, which could be caused by lack of lubrication in the steering system or the steering mechanism of the outboard, and heaviness that manifests itself at speed when turning in one direction rather than in the other. In the latter case the steering is heavier in one direction than the other because of propeller rotation, which is why this condition usually only affects single-engine installations: twin engines with contra-rotating propellers neutralise each other.

With engines of more than 100hp, the steering can be so heavy that you may consider hydraulic steering. Accessory companies produce a variety of systems, some designed for attachment to the outboard itself, some for installation between wheel and outboard. The advantage of a hydraulic system is that it stops the outboard 'pushing' back on the steering wheel—a case of the tail wagging the dog, as it might be. Although feedback is useful, it should be the wheel that dominates the outboard, not the other way round.

Hydraulic systems can be used on single or twin-engine installations, as well as on boats having single or dual-station steering.

Power steering

Two brands of outboards above 200hp currently offer full power steering either as standard equipment, or as an accessory. This uses a hydraulic pump mounted on the engine, operating a cylinder fitted to the steering bracket. The only function of the steering cable is to tell the power system what to do, all steering effort being delivered by the engine-driven pump; it therefore has the disadvantage that there is no feedback at all.

Dual station steering

Larger boats, especially those with flybridges, often have two steering positions. The main problem with dual stations is that they demand long control and steering cables. If not kept well lubricated, these become very heavy to operate, and may stick fast. The cables ought therefore to be kept as short as possible while avoiding sharp bends, which place an unnecessary load on the cable. Greasing the cables at least once a season should keep their action smooth.

Steering difficulties can be overcome by using a hydraulic system. If the throttle/shift controls are too heavy, one solution is to use one of several electronic engine controllers now available, bearing in mind that such systems are designed for larger sterndrive or inboard cruisers, and are priced accordingly!

REMOTE CONTROL

Single-lever

Most electric-start outboards, and all models of 20hp or more, come equipped with a remote control box. The single-lever box combines throttle control and gearshift in one lever; by far the simplest and safest box available, it can be used to good effect with all but the smallest of outboards. Some people would argue that a single-lever box is an extravagant extra on small boats, such as inflatables or dinghies with motors of 15hp or less, but it has to be said that it gives a safety factor, reducing the chance of a boating accident, that far outweighs the additional expense. It is all too easy in an emergency for someone to pull the wrong lever, and go astern instead of ahead.

The single-lever box also takes more care of your outboard. It prevents shifting gear at too high an engine speed, it limits the engine speed in neutral, and yet allows you to apply extra throttle when required to warm up a cold engine. Some deluxe models also incorporate a lock preventing unintentional gear engagement.

Twin-lever

Preferred in some leisure markets outside Europe, the two-lever control is still widely used in racing applications, where a light throttle control is required. The large binnacle controls, each with two levers, give an almost aircraft-type look to the cockpit—especially in twin, triple or quadruple installations. Nevertheless, although appearances are important, the single-lever control is rather more practical for most applications.

Foot throttle

Standard equipment for circuit racing boats, the foot throttle is occasionally fitted in sports runabouts. A single-lever remote control is retained for the gearshift, but engine speed is controlled by means of a pedal throttle. This consists of an aluminium die casting, specially made for the job, and comes complete with connections for the throttle cable. It is spring-loaded so that the throttle closes automatically when released, and therefore you don't have the convenience of hands-off operation. But if you are not concerned with this point, the foot throttle does give a touch of originality to a sporty boat.

INSTRUMENTS

Instruments show what is happening in and around your outboard, and its relationship with the boat. The better the instrumentation, the more information you get; and the better informed you are, the sooner you will be aware of anything going wrong. As with most machines, identifying a problem sooner rather than later will reduce the consequent damage, and cut the cost of repair.

An array of instruments may look impressive, but don't overdo it: an excess of gauges will be too much for the eye to take in, and developing faults may go unnoticed. Fortunately, many of today's outboards, especially the large ones, have a built-in electronic monitoring system to tell you if something isn't right. Suzuki even have speaking outboards that tell you in a choice of languages what is wrong!

Tachometer

The single most important instrument for an outboard motor is the rpm indicator, or tachometer to give it its correct name. No other instrument

Fig. 34. A well laid-out instrument panel with remote control levers conveniently positioned.

indicates how the outboard is running. On small inflatables where it is impractical to fit a tachometer permanently, there are very simple and inexpensive vibration tachometers on the market such as the Treysit (address in Appendix E), which can be used from time to time to check the rpm.

It is important to know how to read a tachometer. We will go into this in further detail in Chapter 4.

Speedometer

Two systems prevail for measuring the speed of outboard boats through the water. First, there is the pressure (or pitot) meter, which measures the pressure of water at the sensor and converts it into a speed. It is rather inaccurate at low speed, but is simple to fit, is reasonably priced, and is usually matched in appearance to the tachometer. Some outboards even have the sensor built-in to the outboard's lower unit, so that you don't need to fit a separate sensor to the boat. Occasionally the plastic pipe between the meter and the sensor becomes clogged, but the blockage can be cleared easily with a blast of compressed air.

Greater accuracy at all speeds can be obtained by fitting an impeller type of speedometer. This works on the same principle as a log, which tows a specially calibrated propeller through the water. Its rotational speed is measured electronically, and converted to speed through the water which is then shown on a meter.

Owners of displacement boats have the choice of a third speedometer type, which measures the rotation of a paddle wheel. This too is accurate at low speeds, but is unsuitable for high-speed craft.

Water temperature

The cooling water temperature is measured by a sensor sited in the water jacket of the cylinder head, or both cylinder heads in the case of V-block engines.

The temperature varies quite considerably according to throttle settings; unlike a car's, this is due not so much to the thermostat as to the pressure release valve that most outboards have in the cooling circuit, which closes at low engine speed to keep the engine warm at idle.

A water temperature gauge is highly overrated as an instrument, and will often give a false sense of security. The most common cause of overheating is a sudden blockage of the water inlet: if you run at full throttle over a plastic bag, the flow of coolant may stop immediately. If this happens, the cylinder temperature will rise so rapidly that your engine is likely to sustain substantial cylinder/piston damage before the temperature gauge even shows that something is badly wrong.

To get round the problem, many of the more progressive outboard manufacturers fit sensors in the cylinder heads to drop the engine speed automatically should the cooling system fail.

Water pressure gauge

A much better indication of the functioning of the cooling system is provided by a water pressure gauge. Here the needle will drop back to zero and the alarm sound the moment the flow of coolant ceases, giving you time to shut down the engine before it is damaged.

The pressure release valve mentioned above, opening and closing to maintain engine temperature at low speeds, will cause large and sudden fluctuations in the indicated pressure. It is important not to misinterpret this.

Some outboard brands have a cooling water flow detector in the engine, coupled to an automatic monitoring system, making a water pressure gauge superfluous. As soon as the detector signals a malfunction of the cooling system, the monitor automatically cuts engine speed, until the defect is rectified.

Ammeter

Essential to check that the battery is charging, an ammeter measures how much current is flowing into or out of the battery. It does not show if the battery is fully charged or not, which is better displayed by a voltmeter. There is little point in fitting an ammeter to an engine with manual start.

Voltmeter

An optional rather than an essential piece of kit, the voltmeter is nevertheless extremely useful. It provides the simplest means of checking the level of charge of a battery. The only other way to find out whether the battery needs charging is to measure the specific gravity of the battery acid with a hygrometer, a fiddling and troublesome task at the best of times. It is better to incorporate a voltmeter right from the start and avoid problems.

Power trim indicator

Power trim indicators are rarely sold on their own, but come as part of the power trim package. They show the angle of the outboard relative to the transom. If the prop is down as far as it will go the outboard is said to be 'trimmed in'; if it is raised slightly away from the transom it is 'trimmed out'. By noting the angle at which the boat runs best on trials, it will be easy to recognise the most favourable trim position for a particular combination of boat speed and load.

Engine monitor

More and more outboard manufacturers are equipping their larger models with an electronic engine management and monitoring system. Items such as water temperature, oil levels, engine speed (and many more, depending on the manufacturer) are constantly monitored and checked against preset parameters. If any of the sensors checking the variables detects an irregularity, the engine monitor indicates something is wrong on a dashboard display, and often takes steps to prevent engine damage, for example by reducing the engine speed down to a safe level. The monitor display should be mounted in a conspicuous position on the dashboard so that it can be regularly checked.

Hour meter

Very much an item of personal choice, the hour meter is more popular on larger boats, especially those used for commercial purposes. It not only keeps a check on how often the boat is used, but can be useful in determining maintenance schedules. Boats used privately are estimated to run an average of fifty hours per year, so maybe it's better to omit an hour meter, and not to be constantly reminded just how little your investment is used!

THE FUEL SYSTEM

Fuel consumption

The size of fuel tank(s) needed for a particular boat depends of course on the size of the outboard(s), the pattern of use, i.e. full-throttle or part-throttle, and how long the engine(s) will be in use at a stretch. As a very rough guide, the outboard's power in horsepower divided by two gives an approximate fuel consumption in litres/hr at full throttle, including a fuel reserve of approximately 15%. Half that figure—i.e. a quarter of the horsepower—will give a good all-round or average-use fuel consumption in litres/hr.

As an example: if you are using a 50hp outboard for one hour at full throttle, you will not go far wrong if you assume a consumption of approx 25 litres/hr (5.5 Imp gallons/hr). For general use (driving about, manoeuvring in and out of harbour, water skiing etc.) allow 12 litres/hr (2.6 Imp gallons/hr). Using this rough guide, it is easy to calculate the size of tank(s) that would best suit the way the boat is used.

Separate fuel tanks

Metal tanks   The outboards at the bottom of the range have integral tanks, and it is usually only above 3hp that separate tanks are offered. The standard small outboard tank is of pressed steel construction, with a capacity of 12 litres (2.5 Imperial gallons). Above 8hp the larger 23-litre/5-gallon tank is standard. Inside the tank a float operates a fuel gauge, and a gauze filter/strainer at the end of the fuel pick-up pipe keeps the sediment out of the fuel lines.

Steel tanks inevitably get scratched or chipped, and in no time, in a salty atmosphere, rust and look unsightly. It is also all too easy to chip the gelcoat or dent woodwork when manhandling a full tank. In addition, an unsecured tank can move about in the boat, affecting stability, scratching the surface the tank is sitting on and, in the case of inflatables, spoiling the wooden floors. Special clips are offered by most manufacturers to clip the tank to the floor, preventing movement.

A refinement of the conventional tank is the Accumix, made by OMC. This consists of two compartments, one for petrol and the smaller one for oil. The oil and fuel are poured into their respective compartments, and the oil is metered automatically to a 50:1 mixture with the fuel (see Figure 35).

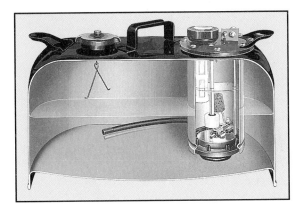

Fig. 35. OMC Accumix (cut-away) fuel tank.

Plastic tanks Although regulations in some countries limit their use, plastic tanks are increasing in popularity, and are already offered as standard equipment on some brands. Against their steel counterparts, they have many advantages: they are easier to carry, they do less damage to your leg, boat or car when banging against it, they are lower and are therefore more likely to be able to fit under a boat seat, they don't corrode, and in some cases they incorporate a reserve. The fuel gauge is normally part of the tank cap.

Flexible tanks Used in the aircraft industry for decades, flexible fuel tanks are extremely convenient for marine use, especially on boats where space is at a premium. Taking up no room when empty, they are easy to stow on board, more or less anywhere. Also, being handy to carry, they don't damage the boat or you. They are the most practical type of tank for inflatables: the only real disadvantage is that their variable shape means that they cannot be fitted with a gauge, although looking at or feeling the tank will usually provide experienced owners with a reasonably accurate idea of its contents.

Safety tanks Safety-conscious outboard users may be interested in special synthetic fuel tanks, used by many commercial and military operators. The non-corroding 24-litre tanks are made of a rigid plastic and are fitted with a pressure release valve so that in the event of fire, they will burn rather than explode (supplier address in Appendix E).

Built-in fuel tanks

Provided tanks can be filled up directly from the pump either at a garage if the boat is trailered, or afloat at a marina, the built-in tank is by far the most convenient to use. The greater capacity means that you will not have to fill up so often, and you will have less spillage, and won't have to manhandle heavy tanks around the dock. Most outboard manufacturers offer matching fuel gauges for built-in tanks.

The most common material for built-in tanks is steel, although some are glassfibre. It is essential that fuel tanks are professionally made, and meet the regulations applicable in the country of use. Special care must be taken with glassfibre tanks to ensure that the inside surface in contact with the fuel does not contain compounds which will dissolve and clog up the carburettor.

Over time, water and sediments will accumulate at the bottom, so there must be some means of draining this off periodically. A fuel cock must also be provided where the fuel pipe exits the tank.

Fuel lines

The fuel line supplied with the outboard is sufficient for most applications, but if you are using more than one outboard or tank different arrangements will be required. Connecting several tanks to one outboard is best done using a two- or three-way fuel cock that allows each tank to be manually selected in turn. Without such an arrangement it would be necessary to disconnect the fuel line from one tank, and reconnect it to another ... an easy job in the showroom, quite another task with a sea running. If more than three tanks are frequently used, then a built-in or large flexible tank would be more convenient.

Fuel lines for built-in tanks usually consist of copper pipes from tank to the transom, and then a length of flexible tubing incorporating the primer bulb. It is a good idea to include, somewhere in the fixed fuel line, a water separator and extra fuel filter.

THE ELECTRICAL SYSTEM

Lighting coils & alternators

Outboards use different methods of producing the electricity they need to run themselves and other onboard equipment: lighting coils, charge coils, alternators, to name but three. Standard on most outboards from 6hp, optional from 4hp, these devices have a voltage output that varies with engine speed unless it is stabilised either by a voltage regulator or by a battery.

The most common rating is around 80W at 12V: some brands give more, others less. It is important to realise, though, that this is the maximum output. What few handbooks or brochures say is that at idle or at partial throttle, e.g. when cruising along a canal, the coil or alternator might only be producing a very small charge, or even none at all.

Another important consideration is the balance between the output power of the lighting coil and the power consumed. For example, using the rating above, if only 60W of lights are connected to an 80W lighting coil, then at full throttle more than 12V will be developed, which could blow all the light bulbs! The remedies are either to match the bulb powers to the coil output, fit a voltage regulator, or connect the coil to a battery via a rectifier. The latter choice gives you the advantage of being able to store power and supply it to the lights later, even if the engine is idling. It is therefore the best solution, especially where navigational lights are concerned.

Electric-start outboards usually have a rectifier as standard, and many larger models also incorporate a voltage regulator to prevent battery overcharging.

Batteries

Single-engine installations A number of battery manufacturers make special batteries for boats; among the distinctive features are a convenient carrying handle, and the fact that they don't spill acid if they fall on their side. Such units may cost more than you are used to paying for your car battery, but you only need to drop a battery once or spill acid over the bottom of your boat to appreciate the marine version's features.

The correct minimum battery size for every outboard will be stated in the engine owner's manual. If the battery is too small for the engine, it may be overcharged or 'cooked' because the charging current of an outboard is not as accurately regulated as in automotive applications. As a rough guide, for outboards below 40hp a capacity of 40Ah is sufficient: larger outboards will require 70Ah, which should be increased to 100Ah for rigs used in cold climates.

Twin-engine installations Twin installations should have two batteries, one for each outboard. Although it is possible to use one large battery, with the alternator of only one outboard connected, this will take away one of the most important benefits of twin engines, that of reliability. (Incidentally, two outboard alternators must never be connected to the same battery, otherwise they will interfere with each other.)

Even greater reliability can be achieved by following the practice adopted on larger boats. Here two batteries are used, each charged independently by one outboard. Both starter motors are connected to the same 'starter' battery, while the second battery is used to supply the electrical equipment of the boat. Isolating diodes (electrical 'one way valves') connect the batteries so that electricity can flow into, but not out of, the starter battery. This apparently complicated system has the advantage that even if the second battery is completely run down—because you've left the fridge on for two weeks, for example—the starter battery will still remain full, ready to start up the engines. Some larger outboards come equipped with isolating diodes for a two-battery arrangement.

RFI suppression

The increasing popularity of VHF transceivers, portable phones, CB radios, echo sounders etc., on board today's outboard-powered boats has increased the occurrence of Radio Frequency Interference (RFI) problems. The effective suppression of RFI can be a daunting task, as adding suppression equipment to the high-tech electronic systems found on today's larger outboards can affect their operation. The most common difficulties and their remedies are described below, but it would be prudent to discuss any problems and intended solutions with the dealer.

Most RFI emissions radiate from the spark plug, and can be effectively reduced to an acceptable level by changing the spark plugs to a different type with built-in RFI suppression. It is important to ensure that you change the type for an exactly equivalent one so that the heat range, i.e. the performance of the part inside the combustion chamber, is not affected. Suppression is achieved by a resistor or inductor within the insulator, denoted on the plug code number by the addition of the letter 'R' for resistor, or 'Q' or 'Z' for an inductor. Which type to fit depends on the ignition system, and will be specified by the manufacturer. Many outboards, especially those built in or for Europe, have these special plugs fitted at the factory.

Additional suppression can be obtained by fitting metal shielded spark plug caps, although these can lead to other problems, such as misfiring, in the salty marine environment.

Another potential source of RFI is the voltage regulator, but its suppression is more specialised, and the manufacturer's advice should be sought.

CORROSION PROTECTION

Sacrificial anodes

Most of the castings used in outboards are aluminium, which in a solution that conducts electricity—such as salt water—corrodes quite rapidly unless protected. Outboard manufacturers treat every part likely to corrode with a special protective surface treatment before painting. A further protective primer, followed by the final finish, gives the aluminium as much protection as is possible. Unfortunately these finishes do not give absolute protection, particularly if the surface is damaged.

One of the cheapest and most effective ways of protecting aluminium in salt water is to connect it to a component made of another metal that will corrode in preference. This is what is known as a sacrificial anode. It is essential that anodes are never painted, and they must always make a good electrical connection to the rest of the outboard. If either of these two conditions are not met, the outboard will start to corrode.

An outboard can have several anodes: the main anode(s) requiring regular inspection is screwed to the underside of the AVP, and is often used as a trim tab. Secondary anodes (if used) are fitted to the lowest point of the bracket. Some outboards even have anodes inside the outboard, in the water galleries, but this is exceptional, and your local dealer can best advise you on their maintenance.

For the external anodes, the only maintenance required is to ensure that they are not painted by accident, and that they are replaced when they are more than 50% used up. You will also have to check the earthing straps periodically. These are used to make a good electrical connection between all parts of the outboard. On no account should they be disconnected or broken, otherwise corrosion will start up—for more detail, see Chapter 5.

The MerCathode system

Many years ago Mercury introduced an accessory called MerCathode. It works on the cathodic protection principle, used in industry to protect structures such as quays and drilling platforms. An electronic circuit senses susceptibility to corrosion, and emits a protective reverse current to prevent corrosion before it can start. It is fully automatic, and can be used to protect any outboard or sterndrive. It uses electricity from a battery for its operation, so if used for prolonged periods, care must be taken to ensure that the battery doesn't run down and stop its operation.

4   Propellers

CHOOSING AND FITTING A PROPELLER

What is a propeller?

At its most basic, the propeller simply provides a method of using the power of an engine to move a fluid. There are other methods of doing so, such as the paddle wheel and water jet, but the propeller is by far the most widely-used system on outboards.

If a rotating propeller remains in the same place while the fluid moves past it, we call it a pump. If the propeller is itself allowed to move, we call it a propulsion propeller. In each case, rotation of the prop causes the movement of the fluid. The (propulsion) propeller on ships is often called screw propeller or just screw, because its rotating action through the water causes it to advance just like a screw advances in a piece of wood. If the spiral thread is removed from a wood screw, giving it the smooth sides of a nail, turning it would not produce progress. Likewise, if the screw propeller hasn't any blades, then there will also be no progress: the blades are therefore fundamental to motion.

Merely having blades isn't enough, however, because if they are not set at an angle, they will just churn up the water, and not push water forward or backwards. They must therefore be set at an angle if the fluid is to be moved. The angle is expressed in propeller language as the 'pitch'.

The rotating propeller sucks water in at the front, accelerates it, and pushes it out behind. The resultant effect is called thrust, because following the rule that says to every action there is an equal and opposite reaction, as the water is pushed one way the boat is pushed in the opposite direction. Unfortunately there is no ideal propeller that produces the maximum thrust under all circumstances, which is the reason there is such a wide variety of propellers available for one outboard. Every shape and design of propeller has advantages under a particular special set of circumstances: if the outboard is used for a variety of purposes, as is usually the case, then a certain degree of compromise must be accepted. If this compromise is not acceptable, then the propeller will have to be changed for each intended use: one for cruising, another for water skiing, and so on. The

Fig. 36. Basic parts of a propeller.

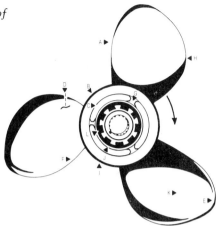

A   *Trailing edge of the blade is that part of the blade farthest from the boat. The edge from which the water leaves the blade. It extends from the top to the hub (near the diffuser ring on jet-prop exhaust propellers).*

B   *Diffuser ring aids in reducing exhaust back pressure and in preventing exhaust gas from feeding back into propeller blades.*

C   *Exhaust passage is the hollow area between the inner hub and the outer hub through which engine exhaust gases are discharged into the water. This is an example of a jet-prop exhaust propeller.*

D   *Blade back is the side of the blade facing the boat, known as the negative pressure (or suction) side of the blade.*

E   *Blade tip is the maximum reach of each blade from the centre of the propeller hub. It separates the leading edge from the trailing edge.*

F   *Cup is a small curve or lip on the trailing edge of the blade, permitting the prop to hold water better, and adding normally about 12.7 mm (1/2″) to 25.4 mm (1″) of pitch.*

G   *Ribs are the connections between the inner and the outer hub. There are usually 3 ribs, occasionally 2 or 4. The ribs are usually either parallel to the prop shaft ('straight') or parallel to the blades ('helical').*

H   *Leading edge of the blade is that part of the blade nearest the boat; that which first cuts through the water. It extends from the hub to the tip.*

I   *Outer hub (for jet-prop exhaust propellers) is the hub area in direct contact with the water and to which the blades are attached. Its inner surface is in contact with the exhaust gases.*

J   *Inner hub contains the rubber hub (described below). The forward end of this hub is the metal surface which transmits the prop thrust, through the forward thrust hub, to the propeller shaft and in turn eventually to the boat.*

K   *Blade face is that side of the blade facing away from the boat, known as the positive pressure side of the blade.*

L   *Shock-absorbing rubber hub is composed of rubber moulded to an inner splined hub. Its purpose is to protect the propeller drive system and to flex when shifting the engine, to relieve the normal shift shock that occurs between the gear and clutch mechanism.*

main factors influencing the behaviour of any design of propeller are described below.

Propeller characteristics

Number of blades   Outboard propellers are usually two- or three-bladed. In the past, two-bladed propellers were more popular, but on today's outboards the three-blade predominates. Generally it is only smaller outboards of up to 5hp that have two-blades, for reasons which we will come on to in a moment.

The greater the number of blades, the greater the propeller thrust area, and therefore the greater the acceleration. Unfortunately, increasing the number of blades increases the drag, slowing the boat down. Decreasing the number of blades, on the other hand, increases propeller vibration. A compromise therefore has to be found, and most manufacturers have opted for the three-bladed propeller.

Small outboards are principally used on dinghies which have to cope with heavily-weeded waters. To prevent the propeller from continually being fouled, they tend to have two-blade 'weedless' propellers. On these the blade geometry is designed so that if the prop hits a patch of weed, the weed slips off the blade rather than entangling itself round the propeller hub. Inevitably this means some compromise, so if the outboard is being used as an auxiliary on a small yacht, where extra thrust is likely to be more important than the weedless action, it would be worth changing the propeller for one more suited to displacement boat applications.

In practice, many external factors influence propeller design, including the number of blades. One example is a specialist sportsboat application like the American bass boats, for which OMC have developed a series of special four-bladed propellers, and Mercury and Mariner a special five-bladed series. These special propeller designs give the high-powered bass boats better acceleration and higher top speed than many three-bladed designs.

This may sound like a contradiction of what we said earlier. To recap, having more propeller blades gives greater thrust, therefore better acceleration. But what about top speed?

Two-bladed propellers theoretically produce a faster top speed than four- or five-bladed propellers because of their lower drag. The reason the special multi-bladed propellers are faster on high-powered craft is that this propeller design gives more lift than normal three-bladed propellers.

The extra lift raises the boat higher out of the water, decreasing wetted surface area. This in turn reduces the hull resistance, effectively increasing the top speed. Trying to run the boat higher would normally cause boat instability (chine riding) but it doesn't happen in this case because these multi-bladed propellers have such a good 'bite' on the water.

The increased drag of the multi-bladed propellers is thus more than compensated for by the reduced drag of the boat hull running higher. This gives a net top speed improvement over a two-bladed propeller running on a hull sitting deeper in the water.

Diameter   The larger the diameter of a propeller, the greater the thrust, but at the same time the greater the drag. Propeller diameter is limited on each outboard by the distance between the propeller shaft and the anti-ventilation plate: for all practical purposes it cannot be changed.

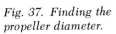

Fig. 37. Finding the propeller diameter.

Measure from the centre of the propeller hub
out to the tip of the blade and multiply by 2.
The diameter is the distance across the circle
made by the blade tips as the propeller rotates.

Pitch   This is the most important characteristic of an outboard propeller. It can be compared to the gear ratio in a car gearbox. When driving a car, you select a low gear for a heavy load, e.g. when accelerating or going up a hill, but a high gear for motorway speeds. Similarly, on a boat you need a low pitch for heavy loads, a high pitch for speed. Just as selecting too high a gear when driving uphill will overload the car engine, using a propeller with too high a pitch will overload the outboard.

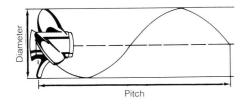

Fig. 38. Propeller pitch.

Fig. 39. Available power
vs rpm at full throttle for
a typical mid-range
outboard.

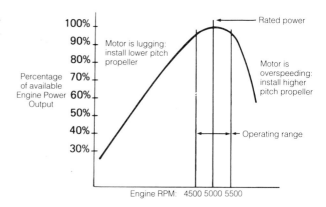

The power developed by an engine depends on the maximum engine speed at full throttle. Fitting a propeller with a different pitch changes this engine speed. If the pitch is too low, the engine will overspeed at full throttle; if it is too high, the engine will not reach full revs, and

Range of engine speed: 4500 – 5500 rpm

Propeller size (in) Dia x Pitch	Material	Boat size Length: metres (feet)	Boat speed					
			150		175		200	
			knots mph	km/h	knots mph	km/h	knots mph	km/h
15¼ x 15	A	6.7 – 8.5 m (22 – 28') Large boats	23–35	45–56	30–36	48–58	32–38	52–61
14½ x 17	A	6.4 – 7.9 m (21 – 26') Boats	32–40	52–64	34–42	55–68	36–44	58–71
14 x 19	A	5.8 – 7.0 m (19 – 23') Boats	36–46	58–74	38–48	61–77	41–51	66–82
13¾ x 21	A	5.2 – 6.0 m (17 – 20') Boats	41–52	66–84	44–55	71–89	48–57	77–92
13½ x 23	A	5.2 – 5.8 m (17 – 19') High performance boats	46–57	74–92	51–63	82–101	54–67	87–108
15¾ x 13	S	Large boats	20–31	32–50	20–32	32–52	20–34	32–55
15¼ x 15	S	6.7 – 8.5 m (22 – 28') Large boats	23–35	45–56	30–36	48–58	32–38	52–61
14½ x 17	S	6.4 – 7.9 m (21 – 26') Boats	32–40	52–64	34–42	55–68	36–44	58–71
14 x 19	S	5.8 – 7.0 m (19 – 23') Boats	36–46	58–74	38–48	61–77	41–51	66–82
13¾ x 21	S	5.2 – 6.0 m (17 – 20') Boats	41–52	66–84	44–55	71–89	48–57	77–92
13½ x 23	S	5.2 – 5.8 m (17 – 19') High performance boats	46–57	74–92	51–63	82–101	54–67	87–108
13¾ x 25	S	High performance boats	52–65	84–105	57–69	92–111	60–73	97–118
14 x 24	*S	High performance boats	60+	97+	60+	97+	60+	97+
14 x 26	*S	High performance boats	70+	113+	70+	113+	70+	113+
14 X 28	*S	High performance boats	75+	121+	75+	121+	75+	121+

1. Material: A=aluminium, S=stainless steel, *S=stainless steel (high performance)
2. High performance propellers can give even better results with the proper transom setting or trim angle.
   Also, optimum rpm is 5500 rpm.
3. Propellers differ in speed from 200 – 350 rpm under same conditions.

Fig. 40. A typical propeller selection chart.

therefore not develop its full power. It is imperative that the outboard runs at the rpm recommended by the manufacturer. If the propeller pitch is such that it cannot, it will only be a matter of time before technical problems—including engine damage—occur.

How can this be checked? Simple: open the throttle fully, and once the boat has reached maximum speed, read or measure the engine speed. If the measured rpm exceeds the manufacturer's stated maximum, fit a propeller with a higher pitch; if it is too low, use a propeller with a lower pitch. As a general guide, increasing/decreasing the pitch by one inch will lower/raise the revs by 200–300rpm. You can use a propeller selection chart (see Figure 40), to indicate the approximate size of propeller for your circumstances.

Rake Rake is the amount the blade is angled off the perpendicular. Most standard props have zero rake, i.e. the blades are set at right angles to the propeller hub axis. Some special propellers are raked up to 20° rearward, so that the blade tips are some way aft of the hub. A raked propeller's improved ability to cope with ventilation and cavitation means that on light, fast boats the outboard can be mounted higher on the transom, improving the boat's performance. Propellers used on displacement boats are not raked.

Fig. 41. Propeller rake.

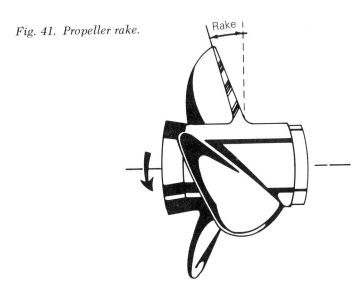

Cupping Cupping is the term used to describe the outward curl on the rear of the propeller blade, similar to the way decorative teacups have a curled lip rather than a straight one. The cup usually gives the propeller a better 'bite' in the water, and improves its tolerance to ventilation and cavitation. This allows the outboard to be mounted higher, and/or trimmed out further, improving a light boat's performance. It has no benefit on slow-moving craft.

Fig. 42. Cupping.

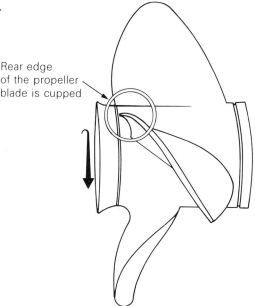

Rear edge
of the propeller
blade is cupped

Propellers are supplied already cupped by the manufacturers. A qualified propeller repair station can usually add a cup to a normal propeller, although this will effectively increase the pitch by 1in, consequently reducing the full-throttle engine speed by 200–300rpm.

Engine output

Horsepower rating The output of an outboard can be measured at different places, and in different ways, giving widely varying values. For example, not so long ago, an outboard model called a '40' claiming to develop 40hp measured at the crankshaft (similar to the SAE method of measurement) produced only 33hp measured where it counts, on the propeller shaft.

Fortunately, output powers are all measured according to the same industry standard ICOMIA 28, which basically means that the output power of the outboard is measured on the propeller shaft (similar to the ISO/DIN method of measurement). Furthermore, the maximum power occurs in the middle of the recommended rpm range, unless it is stated to the contrary.

Engine rpm We have described how changing the propeller pitch changes the full-throttle engine speed (rpm), and that at full throttle, the revs must fall within the band stipulated by the engine manufacturer. A common specification is 4500–5500rpm, but the figure could easily be 5300–5800rpm, depending on the model. The first example gives a 'spread' of 1000rpm, the second only 500rpm.

In practice this means that you can 'prop out' to give full-throttle revs of 4500rpm, 5500rpm, or something in between. In each case the boat will perform differently, but it is important to recognise that the difference will not be limited to speed or acceleration alone: other performance characteristics such as noise, fuel consumption, and engine life will also be affected. Whether the top, bottom or middle of the range is more suitable will depend on the use you intend to put the boat to.

For sports boating, propping out to give an rpm in the upper half of the recommended range with the boat lightly loaded will give a good balance between high top speed and crisp acceleration. The reason the boat should be lightly loaded is that as you increase the load and the engine speed drops, it will still probably remain within the specified rpm range. If you propped out to give a speed at the upper end of the specified range with the boat fully loaded, there is a danger of overspeeding when running light.

Under these circumstances check the revs with a tachometer, and throttle back if the engine is overspeeding. If, in the loaded condition, the engine fails to reach its recommended range, the propeller must be changed for one with lower pitch to avoid possible engine damage.

For water skiing, you need good acceleration rather than a high top speed. To allow the outboard to develop as much power as possible to start the skier from rest, it is usual to fit a propeller with 1–2in less pitch than normal, bringing the rpm up to the top of its specified maximum.

This will give you an 'under-propped' engine, so when not skiing, it will be necessary to keep a careful eye on the tachometer, reducing throttle if necessary to prevent over-revving. The best solution is to have two props, one for skiing, the other for normal use; they only take a few minutes to change round, eliminating the need for compromise.

For cruising, lower sound levels, lower fuel consumption, and lower engine wear are usually appreciated more than maximum acceleration and top speed. It is therefore usual to prop out so that the engine speed lies toward the lower end of the recommended speed band. Bear in mind, though, that your initial boat test will probably not be carried out fully laden, i.e. with all the family and gear on board, so propping out to the middle of the recommended rpm range will allow the engine speed to drop for the fully loaded condition. If the propeller you choose gives an engine speed at the bottom of the band when lightly laden, when you load up the revs will drop so much that the engine will not be able to reach its recommended speed. This overloaded condition is extremely bad for the engine and can damage it in a short period. Watch the tachometer, and throttle back if necessary, until a correct propeller can be fitted.

Workboats have a pattern of use that sets them apart from other motor boats. Part of the time they are empty, part of the time fully laden, and the difference in displacement between the two may amount to several tons. It is essential that workboat engines are propped towards the lower end of the recommended rpm range when in fully laden condition. This will make them over-propped when empty, and their engine speed will soar above the maximum unless throttled back. A tachometer is indispensable in such circumstances, and marking the throttle control for the 'empty' condition serves as a useful reminder to the driver in case he forgets to look at the dial!

Displacement boats, including sailing auxiliaries, need a propeller which will keep the engine speed towards the lower end of the recommended rev range, for the same reasons as cruising boats.

Propeller protection

Small outboards with conventional propellers are fitted with a shear pin between the propeller hub and the shaft. Should the propeller catch on an underwater object, the pin shears, preventing or at least limiting damage to the propeller or drive train. Once the obstruction has been removed, the shear pin can be replaced, and the journey continue.

Larger outboards—about 5hp plus, though it varies from range to range—and outboards with through-hub exhausts dispense with the shear pin in favour of a rubber bush that acts as a form of clutch. Under normal circumstances the bush will transmit drive from shaft to propeller, but if the prop is obstructed it will slip, again preventing damage to prop or drive train. As soon as the obstruction is removed and the propeller is free to rotate once more, the bush will re-engage.

The advantage of this system is that you do not need to replace a shear pin before continuing on your way. Its disadvantage is that once the bush has slipped it is likely to do so again when a heavy load comes on the propeller, i.e. at full throttle. If this happens the only solution is to send the prop to a specialist to have it re-bushed.

Propeller guards   Boats regularly used in shallow water or near swimmers, such as rescue craft, should have outboards equipped with a propeller

Fig. 43. Propeller guard.

guard. The simplest type is an aluminium ring that fits round the propeller, giving it full protection against submerged objects.

It is important to recognise that ring-type propeller guards only give limited protection to people in the water; it is still quite possible for an arm or foot to get sucked into the blades. For complete protection you can buy a cage that fully encloses the propeller, virtually eliminating any possibility of injury.

Propeller types

Conventional   It is no coincidence that the conventional type of propeller is usually found on the small models (up to 5hp) destined for leisure use, and on commercial-use outboards up to 40hp. The advantage of the conventional propeller over the through-hub prop is that it is cheaper to make, easier to repair, and produces higher reverse thrust. This last aspect is important on displacement boats, as reverse thrust is essential for braking effect.

The main disadvantage of this type of propeller is that with the exhaust so close to the surface of the water, if the outboard is mounted too high, the exhaust will discharge straight into the air without any silencing.

Through-hub exhaust   The through-hub exhaust offers the advantage that as long as the propeller itself remains underwater the exhaust will also be below the surface. The only real drawback of this type is that the exhaust has to be ducted away from the propeller blades.

In forward gear, this is done by the diffuser ring fitted to the rear of the hub. If the ring becomes lost or damaged, as sometimes happens when carelessly removing the propeller nut, exhaust gases are sucked into the propeller, causing ventilation and consequent loss of thrust.

Ventilation is also likely to be a problem when using reverse thrust, again because the exhaust gases are sucked into the propeller. Although this might not be critical with planing craft, it can create difficulties on displacement boats, which rely on high reverse thrust to bring their heavy

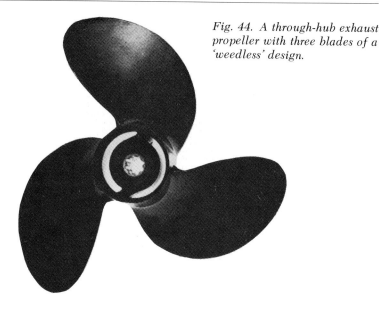

Fig. 44. A through-hub exhaust propeller with three blades of a 'weedless' design.

hulls to a halt: there are, however, ways round this problem, described below.

Some very high-speed boats favour the unusual combination of a conventional type of racing propeller with a through-prop exhaust gearcase. Although this may appear a strange mixture, it is made possible by using special racing props which are designed to run so high that they are breaking the water surface.

Variable pitch Although common on larger ships, variable-pitch propellers—which allow you to move to a higher or lower pitch without the bother of changing the prop—do not yet appear on any outboard manufacturer's list of standard or optional equipment.

The true variable-pitch propeller has the distinct advantage that its pitch can be altered while the boat is underway, ensuring that you have the propeller exactly matched to the present use. Pitch is controlled from the helm position. Unfortunately, so far only inboards and a special sterndrive can be fitted with this type of propeller.

Until variable pitch becomes an option, the closest you can get to it is the adjustable-pitch prop. Here the pitch is altered by turning a knob or screw on the propeller, which means it can only be adjusted when propeller and boat are stationary. If you want to go water skiing, the pitch can be reduced to give faster acceleration: after skiing, the propeller's pitch may be readjusted back to the cruise setting. If the boat is more lightly loaded than usual, the pitch can be increased to reduce the engine speed to within the recommended rpm, and give the boat a slightly higher top speed.

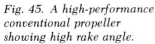

Fig. 45. A high-performance conventional propeller showing high rake angle.

A pioneer of this type of propeller is Technomarine (see address in Appendix E). A further advantage of the system is that, because the blades are separate from the hub, they can be replaced individually in the event of damage.

High reverse thrust We mentioned above that one of the principal drawbacks of the through-hub exhaust prop is its poor performance in reverse. This is because in forward gear the propeller leaves the gases behind it as it travels through the water. In reverse, however, it draws the gases back into the blades, losing a great deal of thrust.

On a planing hull, this is no problem, because as soon as the throttle is cut the boat comes off the plane and stops relatively quickly. A displacement hull is heavier and therefore has greater momentum when under way. The boat will continue on long after you cut the throttle, more or less at the former speed, until you apply reverse thrust to stop it.

The Dualthrust propeller from Yamaha is specially designed to remedy this problem. Being developed exclusively for low-speed displacement boats, the propeller blade shape is optimised for low speeds in reverse as well as in forward gear. Exhaust gases pass through the hub in the normal way in forward, but are ducted away from the blades in reverse (see Figure 46).

One way of modifying a propeller to improve its reverse thrust is to fit a Finze Thrust Booster Kit. This device closes off the through-hub exhaust passage as soon as the propeller starts to rotate in reverse, so that the exhaust gases escape between the propeller and the lower unit, avoiding the

Fig. 46. Yamaha Dualthrust propeller, which pushes the exhaust gases out ahead of the propeller when in reverse to prevent loss of thrust while manoeuvring astern.

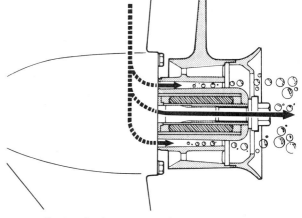

Route of exhaust gas at forward

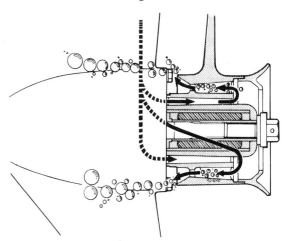

Route of exhaust gas at reverse

propeller blades. In this way you get the full reverse thrust of the outboard without having to buy a new special propeller.

Propeller materials

Aluminium The most common material for propellers' is aluminium, usually die cast and hand-finished before painting. Aluminium props are adequate for day-to-day use: if they are damaged, they can easily be repaired by a specialist propeller repair workshop, who will be able to fit a whole new blade if required. A specialist will also be able to alter the pitch of the propeller, although only by about 1–2in; more drastic changes will demand a new propeller.

Not being as strong as stainless steel, aluminium props tend to have thicker blade sections, which reduces their efficiency.

Plastic   Plastic props have been used for years for torpedo propulsion, but after their initial introduction on outboards up to 20hp during the 1970s, their popularity was limited. Most of today's smallest outboards have plastic props as standard, and with many brands you can specify them as an option on engines up to about 6hp. Their principal advantages are that they cannot corrode, and are less likely to break on striking an underwater object. But they are hardly cheaper than aluminium props, which gives little incentive to change over.

Stainless steel   Although bronze is still widely used in inboards, stainless steel has now replaced it as the material for performance outboard propellers. The superior strength and ductility of steel has allowed the propeller designer to produce shapes and blade thicknesses which have revolutionised propeller technology. Some stainless steels are up to five times stronger than aluminium, permitting very fine blade sections.

Stainless steel props can thus be relied upon to perform better than aluminium ones. Their only real disadvantage, apart from weight, is that they can cost up to three times as much as aluminium propellers!

Ironically, non-corroding stainless steel can actually increase corrosion of the aluminium components of an outboard; boat owners are usually recommended to improve their engine's corrosion protection if they are using a stainless steel propeller in salt or polluted waters.

Propeller problems

Karmann vortex   This somewhat perplexing term is the name given to propeller blade vibration, heard as a 'singing' at particular water speeds, rather like the noise of wind passing through overhead telephone lines. It is a common occurrence, and can often be heard on large ships.

The cause is turbulence at the rear of the propeller blade. If the blade is too rounded, it will introduce vortices that in turn make it vibrate. The cure is to take a file, and put a 45° bevel on the forward-facing side of the trailing edge of the blades.

Cavitation   This term is often erroneously used to describe ventilation, which is something entirely different and is covered in the next section. As we all know, at standard atmospheric pressure water normally boils, i.e. becomes a gas, at 100°C (212°F). At lower pressures, it will boil at much lower temperatures. A propeller turning in water—especially warm water—can set up pressure differences sufficient to do just this, changing the liquid water into gas bubbles.

When the pressure returns to normal the gas reverts to its liquid state: the bubbles 'collapse' back into water. The apparently harmless collapsing of bubbles is in fact very violent, and actually erodes the surface of the propeller blade. Cavitation erosion, or 'burning' as it is sometimes called, can be so severe that eventually the weakened blade breaks off.

Fortunately on an outboard it is easy to keep a check on the condition of the propeller. If cavitation is taking place, the damaged paint surface will give ample warning before any serious erosion can occur.

The two places you are most likely to find cavitation erosion are on the front face of the propeller blade at the root, where the blade joins the hub, and in the centre of the rear face of the blade (see Figure 47).

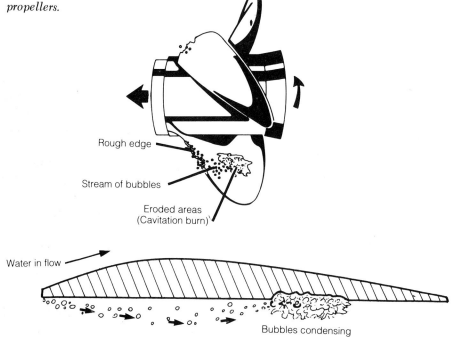

Fig. 47. Cavitation 'burns' on propellers.

Rough edge

Stream of bubbles

Eroded areas (Cavitation burn)

Water in flow

Bubbles condensing

Blade root erosion is caused by the outboard being trimmed too far 'in', i.e. the leg is too far forward. The remedy is simple: move the tilt pin out one hole, or trim out further with power trim.

Erosion in the blade rear centre can be caused by a number of factors. The blade could be damaged, the outboard could be trimmed too far out, or the boat's bottom or the lower unit could be producing turbulence sufficient to induce cavitation at the propeller.

Ventilation   Often confused with cavitation, ventilation is caused by the propeller sucking in air from the surface or exhaust gases.

On planing hulls, ventilation occurs if the outboard is mounted too high, and usually originates in sharp turns, with the propeller losing its 'bite' on the water. In some cases an air ball stays trapped around the propeller; the problem is easy to diagnose, because the engine speed will suddenly increase as the load comes off the propeller. Under these circumstances, the only remedy is to close the throttle to release the air ball, then gradually open it up again. If ventilation in turns is a recurring problem, try using a different propeller that is designed for high-mounted outboards. If all else fails the outboard will have to be lowered.

Another cause of ventilation is exhaust sucked into the propeller. Typical sources are a damaged or lost exhaust deflector at the rear of the propeller hub. Leakage of exhaust through the gap between the propeller hub and the gearcase could also be the cause.

TESTING THE INSTALLATION

It is not always realised that selection of the correct propeller is the most important part of the process of installing an outboard. This is why it is usually left to last, when everything else has been sorted out. Even if the rest of the process has been carried out perfectly, incorrect propeller selection will lead to immediate disappointment and incipient mechanical problems.

After initial installation of the outboard, planing hulls should undergo trials to determine the correct combination of motor height, propeller pitch, and trim tab position. To start with, use the standard propeller delivered with the engine or choose an alternative from the manufacturer's propeller selection chart.

Check that all safety equipment is on board and working, and that there is sufficient fuel and oil (at the correct mixing ratio for running-in if it is a new engine). Adjust the tilt pin to bring the AVP parallel to the boat's bottom. Find an open stretch of water, and run the boat at full throttle, noting the engine speed. Do not over-speed the engine, throttling back if necessary: test for ventilation by trying some moderately tight turns in both directions.

If there is no ventilation, raise the outboard height by 1in or one transom bolt hole, noting the engine rpm at full speed. Place a piece of wood under the clamp brackets to support the outboard better if necessary. Repeat the boat test, raising the outboard progressively until the propeller starts to ventilate; then lower the motor by one step. This procedure ensures the motor is mounted as high as possible on the boat. Fix the outboard permanently in position using the transom bolts.

If the engine speed at full throttle falls within the recommended rpm band (see the Engine rpm section, above), the procedure is complete. If the engine speed at full throttle is outside the band, you will have to fit a propeller of a different pitch to give the correct rpm. Consulting the propeller selection chart, pick a propeller with a greater pitch if you want to bring the revs down, a lower pitch if you want to raise them: a change of 1in in pitch usually represents a change of 200–300 engine rpm. Cupping a propeller effectively adds 1in to its pitch, therefore decreasing engine speed by 200–300rpm.

If you get ventilation in turns even at the 'starting height', it would be wise to consult your dealer, with a view to trying a special propeller.

Having found out which is the correct propeller for your needs, order another one, and carry it as a spare. If the outboard is likely to be operated under different loads, e.g. used for occasional water skiing, the spare can be of a different pitch; this will give you one propeller for light loads, another for heavy loads.

Trials on a displacement boat will normally centre around prop selection, since the outboard should have been mounted as low as it will go without being swamped. Run the engine at full throttle, again noting the rpm. Also run the engine in reverse, trying some emergency stops to test engine braking. From the propeller chart, choose a propeller to give the rpm nearest to that recommended. If exhaust is venting to the propeller in reverse, look for one of the special 'sail' designs that ducts the exhaust away from the prop in reverse.

Once the engine has been fully run in and fitted with the correct propeller, carry out a final test to check that the full-throttle rpm is as it should be. Boat speed should be the same as on the previous test, or slightly higher. If much time has elapsed between the tests, make sure that the hull bottom is clean and not fouled with weed.

5   *Looking after your outboard*

PRE-DELIVERY INSPECTION

In an ideal world this section wouldn't be necessary, as it is the selling dealer's responsibility to carry out a pre-delivery inspection and service. This PDI may, however, be omitted for any one of several perfectly legitimate reasons, in which case you will have to carry out your own check.

All outboard manufacturers check out every motor in a test tank after it leaves the assembly line, fitting larger outboards with a test or load propeller before they are put in the test tank. The motor is started up and its main functions—throttle and choke operation, water circulation, gear-shift etc.—checked. Carburetion and ignition timing are adjusted.

Finally the motor is run up to full speed and the rpm noted as a check that it is developing its full power. On successful completion of final testing, rust inhibitor is sprayed into the engine through the carburettor. The test propeller, if fitted, is removed, and fuel is drained from the carburettor. Protective mats and preformed styropore are put over the flywheel before the top cowling is fitted. The outboard is then packed ready for shipment, with its owner's manual, fuel tank, transom bolts, etc.

On arrival at the dealer's, the engine may remain in store until sold, or it may go straight to the customer. Either way, the dealer should carry out a PDI before he hands the engine over. The purpose of the PDI is to:

1. Check the engine for transport damage;
2. Check that all the bits and pieces that should be there are in fact there;
3. Remove all packing, etc., added to protect the engine during transportation;
4. Prepare the outboard for use by checking the oil level in the gearcase;
5. Start and run the engine in a test tank to disperse any storage oil or rust inhibitor from inside the engine;
6. Check that all the carburettor and ignition settings are correct;
7. Adjust or re-adjust other items such as the swivel and throttle friction to the correct settings.

The importance of the PDI is self-evident, and if for any reason it was not carried out by the dealer at the time of sale, it should be done before the engine is run for the first time.

RUNNING IN

Fortunately, an outboard does not take very long to run in: usually a period of 10–20 hours is sufficient, depending on the model. During this period, it is important that the engine is not run at the same speed, either low or high, for long periods.

Extended running at full throttle should also be avoided, although occasional bursts up to full speed are beneficial to the engine. Brief operation at full speed for propeller selection will not do any harm. I have seen more engines damaged by over-cautious running-in than by being run-in carelessly or not at all!

During running-in, two-strokes should be fed double the usual amount of oil; on outboards using premix, you simply double the oil dosage, and for outboards with automatic mixing, fill the tank with a fuel/oil premix of 50:1 instead of pure fuel.

Each manufacturer will detail specific recommendations in the owner's manual. These should be followed.

FUEL AND LUBRICANTS

Fuel

Whether you should use regular or premium fuel will depend on the design of the engine, the carburettor, and ignition settings. If the outboard is designed for premium fuel, it can be changed by the dealer or importer to run on regular, but there will be a power penalty. If the outboard is designed to run on regular fuel, using premium grade will bring absolutely no benefits, and is just a waste of money.

There is a wide variation in fuel quality throughout the world, so if you are taking your boat abroad, and normally use regular fuel in your home country, it may be necessary to upgrade to premium when you get where you are going. Depending on the destination, it may even be necessary to detune the engine so that it is more tolerant of poorer-quality fuels.

Much confusion exists about lead-free fuels, and whether they are safe to use in outboards. Unleaded fuel can damage some four-stroke engines, for example by causing valves to stick to their valve seats, but not four-stroke outboards, which have non-stick valve seats. It cannot damage two-stroke engines, which have no valves.

Nevertheless, unleaded fuels can cause problems in some older outboards. Lead helps keep the fuel quality high, so some fuel companies put non-lead additives, such as alcohol, in the fuel to boost its quality. It is these additives in lead-free fuels that sometimes create difficulties. The plastic parts of some of the older outboards made in the pre-unleaded days can be dissolved or damaged by lead-free fuels. The type of additives used also varies widely from country to country, so to be on the safe side, if you have an outboard from the pre-unleaded era, stick to leaded petrol when abroad.

Expert advice on a particular outboard, its year of manufacture, and which type of fuel to use, is available from the importers. They have specifications of each outboard, and can advise you with certainty what to do.

Engine oils

The two-stroke outboards of today are technically far remote from the smelly, smoky, and oily two-strokes of yester-year, yet many of the images of these relics still prevail in the minds of the unenlightened. One of the developments which has made the modern two-stroke outboard possible has been the tremendous strides taken in lubrication technology.

Previously, providing the engine with sufficient lubrication under all circumstances was rather a hit-or-miss affair, and so as not to miss, the inside of the engine was saturated with oil to ensure that no vital part was without sufficient lubrication. Inevitably the unused oil either fouled the spark plugs, left a film of oil behind on the water surface, or escaped through the exhaust, partially burnt, in a trail of blue smoke.

The modern approach—providing the engine with just enough top-class lubricant to do the job—includes recirculating oil not used the first time it entered the engine. During the 1970s, in response to the growing ecological awareness especially in the USA and West Germany, a lot of research and development effort went into improving internal combustion engines and reducing their impact on water quality.

Originally, two-stroke fuel/oil ratios were 10:1, and remained so up until the Second World War, during which ratios increased towards 15:1. The 1950s saw a further improvement to 25:1, which prevailed until the mid 1960s, when manufacturers gradually adopted the standard that we still have today of 50:1.

Redesigning many internal engine parts and stipulating a high-specification oil allowed the engine manufacturers to improve on the original 50:1 ratio to produce 100:1 outboards, which were first introduced by Yamaha in 1977. Since then, with automatic injection, ratios of 200:1 have been achieved.

The main properties required of an outboard motor oil are:

What it should do

- mix easily in fuel
- protect against corrosion
- degrade biologically
- be suitable for injection

What it shouldn't do

- cause exhaust blockage
- foul the spark plugs
- leave deposits in the combustion chamber
- cause piston seizure

All outboard engine oils strive to meet most of the above criteria: some do better than others. To make it easier to identify the oils that have these properties, the Boating Industry of America (BIA) many years ago laid down specifications and test procedures which outboard oils must pass to gain their approval. Taking over the work of the BIA, the American NMMA (National Marine Manufacturers Association) is now the leading body to approve outboard oils.

The lower oil classification, TC2, is a low-ash oil suitable for air-cooled and small outboards under 10hp. The more important oil specification is the TC-W, designed for water-cooled outboards running at a minimum ratio of 50:1. The TC-W oil specification was very much the industry standard and provided a benchmark for comparison of new oils, specially developed for specific purposes.

The introduction of oil injection pumps to outboards during the 1980s, however, made it necessary to include an additional requirement for outboard oils. The new requirement was that oils should have a viscosity that would permit injection, a property previously only associated with four-stroke oils.

In 1988 it was agreed within the industry that a new TC-W II specification replace the original TC-W specification of 1971. TC-W II would reflect the needs of the modern outboard not only in respect of an oil's suitability for injection, but also in its tolerance to higher power outputs, leaner oil ratios and lead-free fuels.

Matching the outboard manufacturers' efforts to improve the harmonisation of their products with the environment, the petrochemical industry began to develop high-quality synthetic lubricants. Having a non-mineral base, these synthetic outboard oils are very much more 'edible' to marine micro-organisms than mineral oils, and are thus designated as biodegradable.

To keep abreast of the latest developments in two-stroke engine lubrication requirements, European and American bodies are proposing to rationalise standards for outboard oils into the following groups:

ISO-L-ETD (TSC-4) Outboard oils (eventually to supersede the NMMA
TC-W II specification).

ISO-L-ETE (TSC-5) Biologically degradable two-stroke oil.

Both of these specifications include suitability for oil injection systems.

Gear oils

Gears in the lower unit of an outboard require a good-quality oil usually
based on the extreme-pressure EP90 series of gear oils.

Changing the gear oil is typically a messy job requiring three hands.
To drain the oil, position a washing-up bowl or similar receptacle under
the lower unit—bearing in mind that the oil will run down the casing
and drip off the bottom of the skeg. Remove the bottom oil screw, then
the top one, and allow the oil to drain out.

To refill with fresh oil you need some method of pumping the oil into
the lower unit, which is why outboard gear oil is packaged in tubes rather
than a can. Oil should be pumped into the bottom hole until it overflows
out of the top hole: it may be necessary to use more than one tube,
depending on the capacity of the lower unit. At this point, replace the
top screw, then with sleight of hand remove the oil tube from the lower

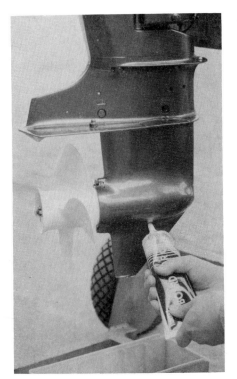

*Fig. 48. Filling the lower unit with gear
oil: squeeze oil from the tube until it
overflows out of the top hole.*

hole, and stick a finger over the hole to stop the oil leaking out: don't lay the tube down on its side if it isn't empty. Then pick up the lower oil hole screw and quickly close the hole. Tighten both screws firmly. Service workshops have special pumps to fill lower units, which makes this job much easier.

Greases

Under no circumstances should greases containing graphite be used anywhere near an outboard. Their use will cause the sacrificial anode(s) to be quickly used up and subsequent rapid corrosion of aluminium parts. All manufacturers supply suitable greases, and their recommendations should be followed.

USING YOUR OUTBOARD

Pre-start checks

Road vehicles make life very easy: you jump into the car every morning, start up, and drive off. Yes, we should check the oil, the water level in the washers, and so on, but few of us do. If something does go wrong, all you have to do is stop the car at the nearest phone and call the breakdown service!

At the other extreme you have aircraft, where pre-start checks involve long detailed check lists and a physical inspection of the aircraft before each flight. A boat will not fall out of the sky if the engine packs up, but neither can you pull onto the hard shoulder and phone for help. So before taking any boat out on the water you should run through a check procedure somewhere in between the car and the aircraft type.

Daily checks should start with a general inspection of the rig. Walk or look round the boat. Are there any loose items lying around? Has someone been tampering with the boat overnight? Has the propeller been damaged? Are all the connections to the outboard secure, including the steering? Is the outboard securely fastened to the boat? Have the clamp screws loosened? Is the safety rope attached? Is the tilt pin in its usual position? Is the boat lying in the water at the usual angle? Is it listing, or lying deeper than usual? In other words, does the boat look right?

Now take a look inside the boat. Is all the safety equipment (see Appendix A) aboard? Check that there is enough fuel and oil, with at least a 15% reserve, for the intended journey. On four-stroke outboards, check the oil level. Is the manual starting rope cut or frayed? Start the engine and immediately check that cooling water is coming out of the tell tale.

Safety first

Do's and don'ts Try to form the habit of tightening the clamp screws before you start your outboard: they do work loose and if not tightened regularly could let the outboard slip over the side in a sharp turn. One way of preventing the clamp screws from loosening is to fit an outboard lock, thereby also preventing theft. But even if you do use such a lock, we cannot emphasise strongly enough the need to check for tightness. Over the course of time the material the transom is made of can 'give', effectively loosening the screws. Transom bolts too should be regularly checked for tightness.

The next item to be checked is the safety rope or chain, whose purpose is to prevent the outboard from going overboard if the bracket does slip.

For many years now outboards over 5hp have had a neutral start interlock to prevent starting in gear. Most systems operate with a cable, which must be kept well greased and adjusted. Always check that the shift is in neutral before starting.

Most outboards also incorporate an adjustable stop to prevent excessive throttle in reverse. Check its operation and readjust if required.

Going back to the 'how used' questions in Chapter 2: if the outboard is likely to be used near people in the water, for example as a rescue boat, it is recommended that a propeller guard be fitted: the cost is not high, and performance is only marginally affected.

One of the best insurances against being caught out by an unpleasant happening is to practise the drill in case it does actually occur. Changing the propeller at sea is one of those jobs that you hope never to have to do; practising it makes it all the more easy when it does happen in reality!

One of the things to be very careful about when changing a propeller at sea is to watch out that the thrust washer doesn't drop overboard. This essential part has a nasty habit of being stuck by grease to the propeller, just as a saucer sometimes sticks to a tea cup. As the propeller is removed from the shaft, plop! The washer slips off, often completely unnoticed. The new propeller is slid onto the shaft minus the thrust washer, and the propeller nut tightened.

The thrust washer ensures there is a running clearance (gap) between propeller and lower unit housing. Without it, the propeller comes so far forward that it touches the housing. In its normal underwater running position, you are unlikely to hear above the engine noise the whine of the propeller grinding away the lower unit. In most cases, when the damage is noticed, it is too late, requiring both parts to be replaced, all because the loss of an inexpensive part went unnoticed.

It is also quite possible to lose the propeller nut overboard. However, this is less of a problem: provided you avoid driving in reverse, the propeller shouldn't come off the shaft.

The other exercise worth trying, though this time in sheltered waters, or even on dry land, is the emergency starting procedure—using a rope wound round the flywheel. This involves removing the cowling, then the flywheel cover, or in the case of manual models the manual starter assembly. It is not necessary actually to start the engine, as this can be done with surprisingly little effort if required.

Never start a water-cooled outboard on dry land: its water pump is lubricated and cooled by the water, so firing up the engine for only a few seconds will usually be enough to burn the pump impeller blade tips. When you subsequently put the outboard into the water and fire up again, there will be an apparently healthy stream from the tell tale suggesting that the water pump is working perfectly; unfortunately what it does not show is that the impeller blade tips have broken off, and may be lodged in a water passage, blocking off cooling to a vital part! The rule is quite simple: never, ever start an outboard out of water.

MAINTENANCE

Preventive maintenance

No one likes to spend more money than necessary, and that applies to maintenance just as much as to anything else. Not doing any maintenance saves money in the short term, only to invite high costs later: preventive maintenance will ensure you avoid those later costs, as well as preventing breakdowns or poor performance that could spoil your enjoyment of your boat.

It is in the interest of every manufacturer that the owner should be satisfied with his or her outboard, so the most appropriate preventive maintenance schedules are compiled from experience by the manufacturers. They are printed, usually as a table, in the owner's manual.

After use: if the outboard has been used in sea water, flush out the cooling system with fresh water to avoid salt crystallising and blocking the water passages; wash down the outside of the outboard to remove salt and sand from the paintwork; spray the engine and ignition parts with a rust inhibitor/water dispersant such as WD40.

If removing the outboard from the boat: loosen the carburettor drain screw if fitted, hold a rag under the hole and drain off any fuel remaining in the carburettor bowl. Keep the outboard in a vertical position long enough to allow water to drain out of the cooling system before laying the motor down. Never lay or carry the outboard at such an angle that its lower unit is higher than the powerhead, or water could run back up the exhaust into the cylinders. With four-stroke outboards, it is important that the engine is laid on the correct side (see the owner's handbook), otherwise oil will pour out of the sump.

Regular maintenance: all the greasing points found on an outboard, as well as the propeller shaft, cables and cable linkages (throttle, shift and steering), should be greased every 50 hours, or every 25 hours in salt water environments. For the average boater doing 50 hours per year in sea water that would mean servicing these items in mid-season, in addition to the annual or winter service.

Winterising

Most owners take advantage of winter to give their outboards an annual service, and while servicing carry out the procedure known as winterising. The name is actually misleading, as if you wait until the onset of winter before winterising you can damage your outboard. For very good reasons, it should therefore be considered an end-of-season service.

During the season, water will enter the gearcase, and it will stay there until drained off with the gear oil. Some models have at least one drain passage in the lower unit which can silt up, preventing the water from draining. As the temperature drops, outboards stored for the winter in a shed or unheated garage can freeze: and as the water in the gearcase freezes it will expand, even a small amount being sufficient to burst outboard castings. Start the winter service before winter, otherwise it may be too late.

Again the owner's manual will give details of specific actions recommended for a particular engine type: the general points are listed in Appendix B.

Corrosion

Most of us have experienced corrosion of one sort, and are familiar with the type of damage it can do to our cars: marine corrosion, basically the same phenomenon, is simply more rapid and vicious. On land, corrosion is usually associated with old objects, but on marine engines it can cause destruction of new components within a few weeks. It can also cause a great deal of damage to your bank balance. Corrosion can better be countered if we understand it, and know what to look for.

Outboards, as we have said, are mostly made from aluminium, partly to reduce weight and partly to protect them from the rust that affects the steel bodywork of our cars. So why do they corrode?

The answer is that they are prone to a far more insidious phenomenon called galvanic corrosion.

A battery circuit is made up of two different metals, connected together by a conductor, in the presence of a liquid that conducts electricity. If such a situation exists, then electricity will flow through the conductor, and one of the metals will dissolve. Which one will dissolve depends on its place in a table known as the Galvanic Table or Activity Series. An edited version of this list is:

Magnesium   *most active*
Zinc
Aluminium
Iron
Steel
Brass
Copper
Bronze
Stainless steel
Silver
Gold   *least active*

Metals at the top of the series are more active than those at the bottom. If any two of these metals are connected and immersed in a conducting liquid (electrolyte), a current will flow, and the more active metal will dissolve.

Outboards are mainly made of aluminium castings (active), and stainless steel shafts (inactive), immersed in water, which, since it conducts electricity, can act as an electrolyte. The parts are connected together electrically, forming a perfect galvanic corrosion cell!

The less pure the electrolyte is, the faster corrosion will take place unless we do something about it. Increased temperature also accelerates corrosion. In other words, warm sea water corrodes faster than cold fresh water. Unfortunately, with an outboard, we cannot do anything about the conducting liquid, so we must find a solution to the problem elsewhere.

'If you can't beat them, join them' is an appropriate way of describing how the outboard manufacturers have solved their dilemma. Instead of having an expensive aluminium casting as the most active metal in the cell, a cheap, expendable piece of zinc magnesium alloy is attached to the outboard, so that it is dissolved in preference to the aluminium.

So long as the zinc/magnesium alloy part, called a sacrificial anode, is connected to the less active metals of the outboard, and remains underwater, it will protect the outboard against corrosion. It is important to recognise that the corrosion hasn't been stopped, it has only been diverted.

From the above explanation, it should be clear that the anode will offer protection to the aluminium if, and only if:

1. It is in good electrical contact with the outboard; and
2. The anode surface is in contact with the water—
   i.e. **not** painted, and **not** lifted above the water surface (e.g. by tilting up the outboard).

Provided these two criteria are met, the outboard will be protected for as long as the anode lasts.

Small outboards usually have only one anode, larger models two or more. The main anode is usually mounted under the AVP, and doubles as the trim tab on models above 15hp. In case the owner leaves the outboard raised, lifting the anode above water, the outboard bracket is often provided with a second anode. Both these should be checked regularly, and replaced when half-worn.

Some outboard models even have anodes inside the cooling passages of the engine and drive shaft housing, but these rarely need to be replaced. If you have to do so, consult your local dealer on this matter.

If for any reason a part of the outboard is no longer in good electrical connection with the rest, then despite the anode operating correctly, that part will no longer be protected and will corrode. As a precaution against this, larger outboards have their main parts connected with small stainless steel earthing straps so that even if the fasteners work loose there will still be effective protection.

Stainless steel propellers or trim flaps accelerate corrosion, and will cause the anode to be used up much quicker, so you will need extra anodes. Using a shore power line at a marina will have the same effect, unless you fit a special galvanic isolator. Corrosion will also be speeded up by copper- or mercury-based antifoulings, which should **never** be used with an

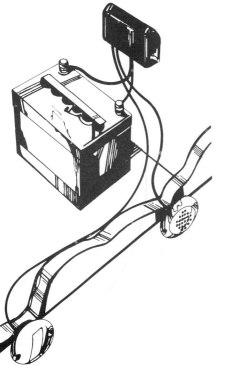

Fig. 49. The MerCathode cathodic protection system.

outboard or sterndrive: only use antifoulings recommended by their manufacturers as being suitable for aluminium drives.

Mercury and Mariner make an electronic corrosion protector called MerCathode which eliminates the need for sacrificial anodes. It works off the main battery and emits a current equal, but in reverse to, the galvanic cell current, thereby neutralising it. Simple, effective and maintenance-free, it provides an alternative solution to the problem of corrosion.

As a matter of routine, any chipped or scratched pieces of paintwork should be dealt with by touching up with a primer and top coat of matching paint. Loose or bubbled paintwork is best scraped or sanded off, rather than using a steel wire brush, whose ends can become embedded in the aluminium and break off to form a perfect mini iron-aluminium corrosion cell.

Submersion

Despite taking all the recommended precautions, such as fitting a safety chain or transom bolts, you may one day be unlucky enough to lose the engine overboard. Don't despair: it may not be as bad as it seems. How you or the workshop deal with submersion, as it is called in the trade, will depend on several factors, including whether the engine was running when it went in, and what happened after it was fished out!

If the engine went overboard still running, water will probably have been sucked in through the carburettor. Since water cannot be compressed in the same way as air can, there may be internal mechanical damage such as a bent connecting rod. Another potential problem will be corrosion.

If the engine went overboard stopped, none of the engine parts will have been damaged mechanically. The only (!) problem to contend with will be corrosion.

While the outboard is under water, salt or brackish water will obviously corrode it faster than fresh. But as long as air is excluded—in other words, as long as the outboard remains submerged—corrosion will be retarded. Even if the engine has been submerged for days, or in fresh water for weeks, all is not lost!

'Above-water corrosion' is a rather cumbersome expression used in the trade to differentiate clearly between what happens when the outboard is underwater, and what happens when it is brought up. As soon as the outboard breaks the surface, the clock is running. In the first hour corrosion will be slow, but thereafter every minute that the engine remains untreated accelerates the damage.

If immediate technical assistance is not available, it is better to leave the outboard underwater until you can organise some help. The worst thing you can possibly do is to bring it up immediately, leave it to dry out overnight and then take it along to the workshop the following day.

As an example, if an engine falls overboard on a Saturday evening and everywhere is shut on Sunday, leave it underwater the whole weekend. On Monday morning, call the workshop to tell them you are bringing in a drowned outboard that will require immediate attention, and then—only then—fish it up out of the water.

Prevention is of course better than cure, but submersion doesn't automatically spell disaster, provided it is properly handled. Outboard racers have been known to suffer submersions and, thanks to skilled mechanics, get back in the race in as little as 12 minutes, still able to finish and even win!

If you wish, or have, to treat an outboard yourself following submersion, follow the procedure itemised in Appendix C.

6 Trailers and trailering

THE TOWING VEHICLE

The modern-day equivalent of putting the cart before the horse would be putting the trailer before the car! It is important, before buying a trailer, to ask whether your car is suitable for the purpose. In general, cars with small high-performance engines are less suitable than those with higher-capacity engines. Automatic transmissions are advantageous, but not a necessity; it is essential that they have a transmission oil cooler, to prevent overheating of the hydraulic fluid when towing for long periods.

A car filled with passengers and pulling the largest trailer its size will allow will weigh almost twice as much as the car on its own with only a driver. The power-weight ratio will effectively be halved, and since the least powerful engine option with most cars is approaching the minimum for efficient performance it is important that your car has one of the larger engine options. A rough guide to the power required is 40hp per ton of total load (i.e. fully-laden car and trailer).

The car also needs to be big enough for the load you want to tow. A safe rule of thumb is to keep the total trailer's laden weight to below 85% of the car's kerb weight—the weight of the vehicle with full tanks, but without driver or passengers, and the minimum of equipment, spare wheel and tools. Expressing it more simply, the maximum weight of the tow should be less than 85% of the car's minimum weight.

The car manufacturer will state what the maximum permitted trailer weight is, taking into account the power of the engine, transmission, brakes and suspension. Failure to keep within these limits not only endangers the safety of the rig, but could infringe the manufacturer's warranty.

The increasingly popular four-wheel-drive car is perhaps also worth considering as a towing vehicle because of its better traction, which can be especially valuable if you have to use a steep launching ramp. Four-wheel-drive vehicles with off-road capabilities will also aid launching and recovery from shallow ramps: their extra ground clearance allows the vehicle to go further into the water, allowing the boat to float off and on to the trailer.

Front-wheel-drive cars give less traction on steep ramps than rear-wheel-drive. The trailer and weight of the car tend to lift the front wheels, while pushing down on the rear wheels.

Towing brackets

The tow bar is equally as important as the trailer, and the safety of your rig will depend on the quality of the tow bar and its ability to do its job properly. If your car is not already equipped with a tow bar, go to a reputable company and have the bar fitted professionally. The standard towing ball in Europe is 50mm in diameter for all trailers up to $3\frac{1}{2}$ tonnes.

The electrical sockets connecting trailer and car are also standardised throughout Europe. There are two types: the normal N-type trailer socket, usually black, with three male and four female pins, and a similar, but slightly different, supplementary S-socket with two male and five female pins. Usually grey in colour, the S-socket is a variant that enables charging of the trailer's battery from the car's generator during driving.

Although mainly used for caravans and other recreational vehicles, the S-socket is a good way of topping up a boat's discharged battery; leaving a battery discharged for a time is one of the best ways to ruin it, but when you arrive home after a day's boating, there are usually other things that take priority over connecting it up to the charger. Then you forget about it, only remembering next time you try to start the engine! Adding this charging facility is an effortless and reliable way to keep the battery charged. A charging relay or diode has to be fitted, to prevent the boat battery from discharging the car battery.

THE TRAILER

Trailer types

As a general guide the dealer selling your type of boat, or the boatbuilder, will be able to give you advice on the type of trailer suitable for each model. If you own a small rowing dinghy, then a simple trailer without brakes or winch may be adequate. At the other extreme, a large runabout or sports cruiser will require a trailer with very much more sophisticated equipment. Where the boat will be launched can also influence the trailer type.

For a great number of boats, the trailer is their home, where they will spend rather more time than they do in the water. The trailer must support the hull adequately, and the rollers and bearers must be adjusted to spread the weight of the hull evenly, over as wide an area as possible. If the boat is not properly supported, the hull can become permanently distorted, with 'hooks' or 'rockers' marring its handling and performance (see Figures 50a & 50b).

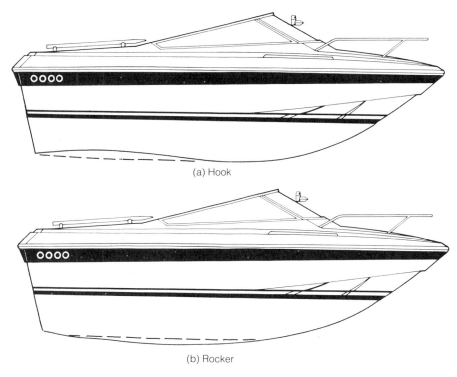

(a) Hook

(b) Rocker

Fig. 50. Hooks and rockers.

Standard trailers carry the boat's weight on keel rollers, with the rest of
the hull bottom supported on straight bearers usually covered with rubber
or some carpet-like material. When the boat is recovered, it has to be
dragged over the bearers and rollers, which is why all but the smallest
trailers are equipped with a winch to make this job easier. Unfortunately
there is no winch at the other end of the trailer to assist launching, and
few trailers can be immersed deep enough to allow the boat to float off,
without at the same time immersing the wheel bearings—something that
is to be avoided if at all possible.

There are two solutions to this problem: the break-back trailer, and the
multi-roller. The break-back, which has been around for some years now,
has a rear section that tilts to allow gravity to ease the boat into the water,
and is invaluable when launching from short ramps.

The multi-roller trailer is a more recent arrival. This has several sets of
large rollers which spread the weight of the hull evenly, so that a simple
push is all that is required to launch the boat. Recovery is also easy, as
there is a special set of gimballed rollers which catches the bows, sliding
the hull into correct alignment with the trailer for an effortless recovery.
Such a design is of course more expensive, but the ease with which it

Fig. 51. A recent arrival to the trailer world is the multi-roller trailer.

operates is really remarkable. This self-aligning-bow feature is offered by some trailer manufacturers on their standard models.

Whether your trailer should have single or twin axles principally depends on the load you intend to carry. If your boat weighs more than 1650lb/750kg all-up you will need a twin-axle unit to keep the loading on each axle to an acceptable level. Inevitably, twin-axle trailers are considerably heavier than their single counterparts, and therefore reduce the load you can carry, but they do give an added safety margin in the form of an extra wheel on both sides. This will be welcome in the event of a puncture, which can be an extremely unnerving experience with a single-axle unit.

Trailer size

Trailer weight has been covered above. Trailer size is another matter, since different regulations come into force with different dimensions. For unrestricted towing with a private car, the length of the trailer plus load may not exceed 7m (22ft 11½in) excluding draw bar, and its maximum width, including load, may not exceed 2.3m (7ft 6½in).

Lights, reflectors and registration plate

Boat trailers must be fitted with two white front (side/parking) lights, two red (side/parking) lights to the rear, brake lights, registration plate lights, direction indicators, a minimum of one rear fog light and two triangular reflectors. If the length of the trailer plus load exceeds 5m (16ft 4½in) yellow reflectors have to be attached to the side of the trailer. The registration plate carried on the trailer must be the same number, shape and size as that carried on the towing vehicle.

Brakes

Although there are some trailers available without brakes, they can only be recommended for towing light boats. Trailers without brakes may be used so long as their laden weight does not exceed 750kg (1650lb) or half the towing car's weight, whichever is less. Braked trailers must have a parking brake, and should incorporate an emergency device to stop the trailer should it become detached from the vehicle towing it. Modern braked trailers incorporate an automatic reverse device to stop the brakes from being applied while reversing. With some of the older designs, still about, you have to manually disengage the brake before you can reverse.

Passengers

Passengers may not be carried in the trailer when it is moving.

Mirrors

A wing mirror on the passenger's side should be fitted when towing a trailer, and is essential if the boat obscures the view in the rear-view mirror.

Tyres

The regulations covering tyre condition and tread depth on motor cars also apply to trailers. Not only must the tyres fitted to the trailer be of the correct size, they must be capable of handling the load the trailer is expected to carry at the speeds expected to be attained. It may be advisable to fit reinforced tyres so that the higher speeds permitted in some foreign countries may be safely maintained. Keep to the same type of tyre: do not mix cross-ply tyres with radials. Keep the pressures correct, checking them while the tyres are cold, before your journey starts.

Most of the life of a trailer tyre is spent stationary, concentrating the load on one spot. If you are not using the trailer for a while, roll it forward or back a foot or so every so often to spread the wear and avoid 'flat-spotting'. During off-season storage, take the load off the tyres completely by jacking up the trailer and resting it on blocks. Cover the tyres with a piece of cloth to keep them dark: this will reduce ozone cracking and prolong their life.

Always carry a spare wheel for your trailer, and check that the jack works: most car jacks will not operate on a trailer.

USING THE TRAILER

Loading

Any superfluous weight carried on the trailer will reduce your car's performance unnecessarily. It makes sense to travel with empty boat tanks, filling up with fuel and water near to the launch site rather than before leaving home. If you book passage on a car ferry, you will usually find you are not allowed to carry a quantity of fuel in anything other than the car's tank.

Moving the boat forward and backwards on the trailer will change the trailer loading. The winch post on the trailer carries a snubber which holds the boat's bow to prevent the boat from moving any further forward, and serves as an indicator that the boat is in the correct position.

Assuming the trailer is the right size for the boat, you can find the correct position of the winch post and snubber by first adjusting it so that when the boat is in the fully forward position the trailer is evenly balanced. The boat should be fully fitted-out, with engine and all equipment installed and fixed in place. Then move the post forward a couple of inches to give the trailer a slightly nose-heavy attitude: you can use a set of bathroom scales to check the load at the front, which should be around 75lb/35kg. The load should not exceed the limits for the car shown in the owner's handbook. A slightly nose-heavy attitude also makes it easier manhandling the trailer on its jockey wheel.

Projecting loads

Very precise regulations are laid down concerning projecting loads, and it is outside the scope of this book to attempt to cover them all: your motoring organisation will be able to give you information on the latest regulations applicable at home and in different countries. The laws most likely to apply to motor boat owners is that the registration plate light board must be within 1m (39in) of the rearmost part of the load—i.e., in most cases, the outboard on the boat's transom. If any part of the load is overhanging by more than 2m (79in) you will have to display an overhang marker board.

A certain amount of common sense is required in marking projections such as masts and outboards: it may be difficult for following traffic to judge the distance between them and you. A piece of red cloth tied to the end of a mast will help and outboards should have their lower units bagged and, if possible, their propellers removed: the sharp edges could cause injury.

Towing for the first time

The first time you venture out on the road with your trailer, try to pick a quiet time so that you are not distracted by other road users. Remember to swing out at corners to avoid kerbing. Your car could be pulling nearly twice its normal load, so allow for a reduction in acceleration, and an increase in your braking distance. As well as being heavier, your car is now effectively much longer, so don't pull out in front of oncoming cars: let them pass and wait for a suitable gap in the traffic.

Try to find a large quiet open space, like a supermarket car park on a Sunday morning, to practise reversing. You will have to become accustomed to the way the trailer turns in response to the car's movements. As with most things, practice makes perfect: try to take the time, because the investment will repay itself many times over in the future.

Snaking

A particularly alarming condition that can arise when towing is snaking, when the trailer begins to weave ever more violently from side to side. Usually caused by excessive speed, it is often first encountered on the motorway, when buffeting from high-sided vehicles produces a cross-wind that starts the process off. Whatever you do, do not apply the brakes, as this only makes things worse! Allow the vehicle to slow down gradually, noting the speed, so as to be able to avoid snaking the next time. Incorrect tyre pressures, and uneven distribution of the trailer load, may also be to blame.

TRAILING AND THE LAW

This section is for guidance only, and is not an attempt to interpret the laws of the country where you will be using your trailer. It is essential that you seek up-to-date advice from your motoring organisation before you start using your trailer on the road.

In most countries a full driving licence entitles you to tow a trailer behind a car; a provisional licence is insufficient. Depending on the country of registration, additional road tax for the trailer may be required. In the UK, no extra tax is payable on trailers intended for private use: if in doubt, check.

Your car insurance policy will usually give limited cover for an attached trailer only. Loads—i.e. your boat—will be excluded, as will the trailer itself when it is unhitched. This should be confirmed with your insurance company. It takes only a few seconds for someone to drive up, hitch up an unlocked trailer and drive off: make sure you are properly insured for on-land mishaps as well as water accidents.

Speed limits and road behaviour

Again your motoring organisation should be consulted, as speed limits vary according to road type and country. In the UK the maximum permitted speed with a trailer is 50mph (80km/h) on normal single carriageway roads; on dual carriageway roads and motorways it is 60mph (96km/h). Remember to heed the special signs for trailer-towing vehicles, especially common on motorways. They limit the lanes which may be used; trailer vehicles are prohibited to use the outside lane of a three-lane motorway, and are often restricted to the slow lane in contraflow systems.

Launch and recovery

On your first launch, don't be afraid to ask another boater to help you. If you are not too experienced, don't be in too much of a hurry, and try to watch how others do it.

It is important to remember that warm trailer wheel bearings and water don't mix. After a drive to the launching site, have a coffee and wait for 30 minutes or more to let the bearings cool down. If the bearings are immersed when warm, air inside the bearing contracts on contact with the cold water, creating a vacuum. Water is consequently sucked in, past the seals, into the bearing, to cause future damage: naturally the situation is even more serious with salt water.

Even better is to effect the launch without immersing the bearings at all. Although not always practical, the break-back and multi-roller trailer do make this possible on a wide range of launching sites.

When you reach the shoreline, tilt the outboard up as high as possible, and untie the retaining straps, keeping the bow winch wire taut. Reverse the trailer into the water to a depth sufficient to be able to float the boat off. If the incline is too shallow for the boat to float off before the back of the car is immersed, tie a rope between the trailer and car, and if necessary push the trailer into the water. Take hold of the painter (the rope tied to the bow), unclip the winch wire, and give the boat a gentle shove to clear it from the trailer. Remove the trailer from the ramp so it is free for others.

For recovery the trailer may have to be immersed deeper in the water so that the boat can be lined up and floated on to the trailer, rather than having to be winched on. The shallower the angle of the ramp, the deeper you will have to immerse the trailer. Stop the engine, raise it as far as it will go, remove your socks and shoes and climb over the side, holding the painter so that the boat does not drift away.

Leave someone in charge of the painter while you collect the trailer and bring it down to the water. Line up the boat with the trailer—using the paddle makes it easier—attach the winch wire to the bow, and winch the boat up onto the trailer, taking care that it remains properly lined up with the keel resting on the centre rollers.

Beware the effect of tides. Most ramps are fine at high tide, but as the tide ebbs they can present a host of difficulties. A common problem is that the ramp does not extend as far as you would like into the water. If you can see the end of the ramp, all well and good; if not, you may find yourself backing the trailer over the edge! Extra hands are usually required to recover the trailer, and if there isn't an alternative ramp locally, patience is required to wait for the tide to come in again.

The other most common difficulty is that when the water recedes it exposes a ramp covered in green slimy seaweed which even a tank would find difficult to negotiate, never mind a car with a trailer. A length of strong rope can often save the day. Pull the car up the slope to a drier patch, and secure one end of the line to the tow bar, the other to the trailer. This should give better traction. As an emergency traction improver, you could also get crew or onlookers to sit in the car or on the bodywork. Bear in mind that the trailer brakes will be less efficient when wet.

TRAILER MAINTENANCE

The usual type of car trailer is very different from a boat trailer: it doesn't need to be adjusted to fit the shape of your hull, and it doesn't have to withstand regular immersion in (sometimes salt) water. The boat trailer thus needs a good deal more consideration and maintenance.

1. All adjustments should be checked regularly during the season to make sure that no bolts have worked loose.

2. Bearings should be regularly lubricated with special grease, in the case of some bearing types following every immersion.

3. Brakes, including the handbrake, require adjustment and inspection during the season.

4. The tow coupling and jockey wheel should be kept clean, well lubricated and free to move.

5. Check the condition from time to time of the various rubber boots used on moving parts of the trailer. If there is any sign of cracking or tears, replace them immediately. Even a few weeks' delay can allow irrevocable damage to set in.

6. The winch has to work hard and can only give of its best if it is properly looked after. That means cleaning and oiling the winch mechanism, as well as looking after the wire. Wind the wire out completely and check that the end is properly attached to the drum: look out for corrosion on the wire and remove any kinks, which are potential breakage points. If the wire is in bad condition, replace it.

7. The rubber rollers supporting the boat should also be in good condition. Replace any that are hardening up or are badly cut.

8. Other moving parts should also receive lubricant to keep them working smoothly. Read the trailer manual or check with the manufacturer of your trailer.

7   *Going boating*

BOATING CLUBS

One of the best ways to learn more about boating is to join a local boating club. The members making up the club have at least one thing in common: they are enthusiastic boaters. You will find them only too pleased to give you valuable assistance and tips on local boating, and they will also be able to give you advice on who are the best dealers in your area, and more important who best to avoid.

Clubs are usually affiliated to the national umbrella boating association such as the UK's Royal Yachting Association. The RYA is not, as its name suggests, concerned solely with yachting and sailing, but with all types of boating, powered or otherwise.

Any boating matters a local club feels they themselves cannot handle can be referred to the national association. These in turn are affiliated with other national associations in other countries, and are therefore able to call on expertise from abroad when dealing with boating matters internationally.

Many clubs run navigational and seamanship courses, which are usually a more effective way of learning than studying in a book, and certainly a more sociable one! An alternative method of learning these subjects, gaining in popularity, is on a computer: many educational programs are available covering the most important boating topics.

Boat insurance

Insurance is another area where your local boat club may be able to give you some advice: they may have a deal with a broker who offers members special rates. Fortunately marine insurance is not as expensive as most other forms of insurance, but it still is worthwhile shopping around for the most competitive premiums.

Apart from wanting to protect your own investment against theft or damage, you will need to include cover for third-party risks. Many boats cost a great deal more than a car, and consequently cost a great deal more to repair if damaged. Injury to a member of your crew, or a swimmer in the water, could also result in a claim against you, so whatever the value of your boat you should ensure that your insurance includes a minimum of £250,000–500,000 third-party cover.

Another aspect of insurance you need to be careful about is coverage during winter, whether you use the boat in the off-season or not. If the boat is to be kept at home it will pay also to check your house policy: having an integral fuel tank full of petrol in a boat is very different to having the same quantity stored in a garage over winter, and there may be a clause that invalidates your house insurance if you store more than a certain amount of fuel. There is also the question of the material of the tank, especially flexible tanks, which may be perfectly acceptable in a boat but contravene building or fire regulations when stored in or near a dwelling.

Some policies may only cover use in the home country, which is of course no good if the boat is trailered abroad each summer. Be careful to watch the small print, and when comparing costs, make sure that the coverage being offered is adequate for your needs.

BOATING AND THE LAW

Driving qualifications

The regrettable annual increase in boating accidents, most of which are avoidable, strengthens the argument for the UK to follow the course many other countries have already taken in requiring their citizens to pass theoretical and practical tests before allowing them to go boating.

The lack of a legal requirement for a licence in the UK does not free the skipper from the moral requirement to be qualified to go boating. Fortunately the waterways are less crowded than our roads, which is perhaps the reason there are not more boating accidents. At least in a car, you can always stop at the side of the road, and wait for the police or someone else to come along and help you; but out at sea or on a large lake, there won't always be someone around to help. So the skipper, at least, must know what he is doing, and must also be prepared to cope with the consequences should something go wrong.

Experience is one of the best teachers, but by definition takes time to accumulate. Following a course of instruction is in effect learning from other people's experiences. Here again the boat club can be of help; if they do not run courses themselves, asking around the club will probably unearth at least one experienced skipper enthusiastic enough to give you some instruction.

Knowing how to handle a boat is by no means all the skipper needs to know. Every skipper, no matter how inexperienced, should be aware of certain basic rules grouped together under the heading of seamanship: the Rule of the Road at sea, which stipulates who has right of way in every conceivable situation, plus other conventions such as the meaning of fog signals, and the shapes and colours of buoys and other navigation marks.

If you intend to make a passage, it is essential to gain an understanding of navigation, and know how to read a chart. Keeping a chart of the local cruising ground aboard is always recommended, and is essential if you are boating in strange waters: merely looking at the water surface can be deceptive and only by referring to the chart can you be sure that there are no underwater obstructions. If you do not take a course in navigation or seamanship, there are many excellent publications in book form or videos suitable for home study. For computer enthusiasts, some of the boating magazines advertise programmed learning software on boating subjects.

If you are living in a country where a boat licence is mandatory, the local boat dealer or club will be able to advise you what procedure to follow to obtain a licence.

If you plan to go boating abroad, first ask your national association about the requirements in force there. If a licence is required, your own boat club may be able to issue you with an internationally acceptable Certificate of Competence, as an equivalent to the licence required in that country. Be sure to allow yourself plenty of time, i.e. several months, as you may be required to follow a course of instruction to qualify for the Certificate.

Some countries issue permits to limit the number of boats on a particular lake or river: boating without such a permit is illegal. Visitors can sometimes obtain day or week permits, but it is best to check this again well in advance: contact your national association for details.

Boat registration

Most countries demand boat registration of one form or the other for all but the smallest craft, although in the UK, surprisingly, registration is only required on inland waterways, where the managing authority will operate an annual licensing system. If you use a British boat abroad you will at least need to register it under the Small Ships Register, run by the RYA. Here again your boat club or national association will be able to advise you.

Construction regulations

Boatbuilders' federations in the major motor boat producing countries— the USA, UK, France, the Scandinavian countries and Italy—have, over the years, developed standards and codes of practice on boat construction which they expect their members to meet. In general, a serial plate indicating that a boat has been built by a member of the federation implies that the boat complies with these standards. Furthermore, boats built in the USA have to carry a US Coastguard plate which clearly shows items like the manufacturer, maximum number of persons the boat may carry, maximum engine power, the boat's buoyancy etc.

A European Community directive on boats and the equipment fitted on them is in preparation, but it is not expected to be active until 1994 at the earliest. With few exceptions all boats and equipment sold in the EC will have to comply with the new regulations, so that boats and equipment from outside the EC will still have to meet these new standards. A serial plate bearing the EC mark must be attached to the boat, proving that it meets the prescribed regulations, which will be backed up by on-site inspections of the manufacturing facilities. The plate will also indicate the boat's limitations as to maximum power, number of passengers etc.

The information given on the plate(s), whether issued by the boat-builder, Coastguard, or other authority, is there for the guidance and protection of the boat owner and crew. Ignoring this information—for example, by over-powering the boat—could bring legal liability problems for the boat owner and even the dealer fitting the overpowered engine, especially if an accident occurs.

Authorities

Contact with authorities will depend very much upon where the boating will take place, and obviously different countries have different requirements. The main points to consider are that the local waterway authority should be contacted if boating on inland waters. At a marina or harbour, talk to the harbourmaster: if leaving or entering a country, contact the local Customs Officer. When making a sea passage, advise the harbourmaster or Coastguard of your planned route, departure times etc., and of course report your arrival, especially if you end up in a different port to the one intended.

SAFETY AFLOAT

Compass

An essential part of the equipment of any boat is a compass. Larger boats will rely on the compass for navigating and steering a compass course; but even smaller boats will find one useful if caught out by mist on a lake, or coastal fog at sea.

If the boat's layout permits, the compass should be mounted ahead of the steering position, as near as possible in line-of-sight of the driver. An alternative is the aircraft type, attached to the windscreen. In both cases, they should be wired into the instrument lighting circuit, so that they can be read at night without having to use a torch, which could destroy the helmsman's night vision.

Make sure you buy a compass suitable for motor boats: many of the compasses designed for the yachting market are insufficiently damped for motor boat use, and would therefore be difficult to read in anything but a flat calm.

When using a compass, remember that iron and steel objects placed nearby will affect the magnetic field and cause compass errors. Even radios, personal stereos, etc., contain magnets, and you need to watch that no one inadvertently puts down some equipment that will cause the compass to give an incorrect reading.

Lifejackets

Not to be confused with buoyancy aids (the waistcoat-like jackets you often see water skiers wearing), a lifejacket should be able to turn and keep even an unconscious person upright so he floats on his back with his nose and mouth clear of the water surface. There are four types of lifejacket: inherent buoyancy, meaning they are pre-filled with buoyant material such as foam, which makes them bulky and awkward to wear on the boat; air-filled, where the wearer inflates them using a mouth tube; air-foam, a combination of the two; and CO_2, which is inflated from a gas bottle, like the jackets used on aircraft. The problem with all the last three is that if the wearer goes overboard unconscious after being struck on the head, they will not inflate. The answer, if you can afford it, is an automatic CO_2 lifejacket, which inflates automatically when the wearer hits the water.

Automatic lifejackets are not recommended for children, so choose a comfortable foam lifejacket or even a good buoyancy aid so that they can wear it all the time: the lifejacket's ability to invert an unconscious wearer is of lesser importance, as there will normally be an adult about to give help.

If you do need all the lifejackets at once, the emergency is likely to be a very real one, so they must be kept where they can be reached instantly. It is useless keeping them stuffed away in a locker that from time to time floods with oily bilge water that rots the jackets, or in one that is so inaccessible that it takes ages to reach.

For some jobs, such as working on the foredeck, or hanging over the stern to change a propeller, it makes sense to play safe and put on a lifejacket. Pleasure boating should be a pleasure, and if an adult feels happier wearing a lifejacket, let him (or her): encourage children to wear a lifejacket at all times.

Distress flares

Many countries demand that craft operating in coastal waters carry a set of distress flares, but whether required by law or not, it is sound common sense to carry a set. They should be stored in a dry and safe place—under lock and key if there are children about, but remember to unlock them when going to sea!

If a boat does get into trouble, a flare provides one of the best means of summoning help. Radio is better, but many breakdowns at sea are caused by electrical or battery problems, which may knock out the radio at the same time as the engine stops. Provided the flares' expiry date is respected, they are completely reliable, and very effective. Also, unlike a radio, no previous experience is required to use them: just follow the instructions. (This does not mean that you should wait till there is an emergency before even looking at them—ideally, you should read through the instructions at least once a year so you are familiar with their operation.)

There are three main types of flare: rocket, handheld, and the smoke float. The rocket flare is designed to summon help by attracting attention: it fires a red flare about 1000ft/300m in the air, and the flare descends gradually on a parachute. The handheld flare is a position-fixer, particularly effective at night, while the smoke float is its daytime equivalent. Being just above sea level, both the handheld and the smoke float can only be seen over a short distance, but search-and-rescue can use them to zero in on a boat or liferaft from a surprising distance away. Flare manufacturers offer sets of flares stored in a waterproof pack, suitable for each application.

Bilge pump

At the lowest end of the range, a bailer and sponge is all that is necessary to remove accumulated water from the bottom of small boats. Larger boats will need a fixed manual bilge pump. If the equipment on board includes a battery, it is worth adding an electric pump: the presence of the battery itself implies that there will be other permanent fixtures on the boat, such as an outboard, which would be damaged if the bilge water were to rise excessively. It is very simple to fit an electric bilge pump with either a built-in or separate switch to operate the pump. With a built-in float switch, as soon as water in the bilges reaches a predetermined level, the pump cuts in and continues to run until the level drops. Because of the possibility of pump and/or electrical failure, a back-up manual bilge pump is a sensible extra.

From time to time boating magazines test electric pumps, and there are always discrepancies, sometimes as much as 50%, between the capacity given by the manufacturer and that measured by the magazine: the manufacturers' explanation for the discrepancy is usually that the magazine has measured the flow in a different way! When buying an electric bilge pump, it is therefore better to err on the generous side and get a larger one than you think you need.

Fire extinguisher

Another advantage of the outboard-powered boat is the reduced risk of fire: there is no engine compartment beneath your feet collecting spilt fuel and volatile vapours, just waiting to catch fire.

Nevertheless, you should always carry at least one extinguisher, kept within reach of the driver, and if there is a cabin, a second one down below. Boat extinguishers should be light enough to be held in one hand—you may need the other to hang on with—and therefore should not be larger than 5.5lb/2.5kg.

The most likely source of fire on an outboard cruiser, in fact, will be the galley. Fire here is best fought with a fire blanket. Not only can it be used in the galley, but is also excellent for smothering a fire on someone's clothing.

The two most suitable types of extinguisher for marine use are dry powder and BCF. Dry powder, which is suitable for all types of fires, produces no fumes and is safe to use in confined living spaces such as the cabin. BCF is a gas and is especially suitable for fuel, oil and electrical fires; unlike dry powder, it leaves no residue, but being a gas it should not be used in the accommodation.

Fire extinguishers for marine use have an aluminium cylinder (domestic ones tend to be steel) which lasts longer in the corrosive marine atmosphere. Most extinguishers on boats are fitted and forgotten about for years and years, until they are needed. They should be serviced as often as the manufacturer recommends; better still, choose an extinguisher with a pressure gauge so that it is easy to check that it is still serviceable.

Radio receiver

As well as providing entertainment value, a radio receiver is also an essential item of safety equipment on any boat used at sea, or even on inland lakes. Before boating, the sensible skipper consults the weather or shipping forecast: most meteorological offices provide a continuously-updated telephone recorded message service, and anyone with teletext on their television has access to another regularly-updated forecast.

But the weather forecast should not simply be something you listen to before deciding whether to go boating. Once you are afloat, keep the radio switched on and tuned in to a station that provides forecasts: even in summer, severe storms can blow up in a matter of hours and without warning can turn a peaceful outing into a nightmare. Forewarned, you have time to get back to harbour.

VHF radio

The modern compact VHF transceiver is being fitted to smaller and smaller boats each year. Many authorities broadcast storm warnings on VHF, and even a portable set will allow the driver to contact the Coastguard or other boats in the area in an emergency or if assistance is required.

Other safety equipment

On board a boat, even a simple thing like a blown fuse can create a difficult situation if there is no alternative light source to let you can see what you are doing in the dark. A waterproof torch and a spare set of batteries are essential on every boat.

A paddle or a set of oars is to be recommended, not only as back-up propulsion in case of engine failure, but also for manoeuvring in shallow waters—such as when you are approaching a trailer. It is surprising how many rocks and boulders there are near a launching ramp, and a cautious approach under oars or paddling could save the unsuspecting boater a chipped or broken propeller.

An anchor is another of those items which, even if you don't need it in the normal course of boating, may one day be needed to play a safety role and get you out of a problem. There are many different types of anchors available, but for normal use a stockless or Danforth type gives good holding for its size and weight, and stows reasonably well. An anchor line 30ft (10m) long should be adequate for most purposes.

USING AN OUTBOARD ON INLAND WATERWAYS

Canal or river cruising brings you up against rules and regulations not encountered on the sea. Many waterway authorities impose regulations on engine installation, the installation and use of toilets and other aspects of the boat's construction. Craft using these waters will usually be required to carry a licence or permit, and may have to pass a technical inspection.

If you are cruising abroad, you will find that some waterways—for example, large European rivers—have their own buoyage system and convention of signals to be shown when passing each other: a good knowledge of them is essential for a safe passage. A misunderstood buoy or failure to heed a signal could have very serious consequences on a busy waterway.

Other considerations, such as speed limits, may influence your choice of outboard for use on inland waterways. There is a growing preference for four-stroke outboards inland, especially where speed limits require them to be run for long periods at low throttle settings. Four-stroke outboards tend to run more smoothly at lower revs than many two-strokes, some of which exhibit a roughness through the 1500–2200rpm band.

Although it is much more agreeable to listen to a larger outboard running at half-throttle all day than a small outboard at full speed, there is a disadvantage. At half-throttle the lighting coil will not be delivering its full charge of electricity, and depending on the equipment aboard there may not be enough to run all the important electrics as well as keep the battery charged.

If you intend to use the boat at night this could present a problem, leaving you insufficient power to run the navigation lights.

Other equipment required for inland boating includes a horn, a spotlight or headlight for tunnels, plenty of fenders to protect the topsides, and adequate cordage in the form of bow and stern lines, plus a length of heaving line.

USING AN OUTBOARD AT SEA

A phenomenon often overlooked by a new owner is marine growth. If boat and outboard lower unit are not kept clean of weed, barnacles etc., the performance of the boat will be drastically reduced, in extreme cases so much so that it can even prevent the boat from planing. Top speed can deteriorate weekly as the growth increases, and often the poor dealer or manufacturer gets blamed for the supposed 'loss of performance'. Use

Fig. 52. Marine growth after 12 days.

Fig. 53. Marine growth after 36 days (we don't dare to show you the picture of what this boat looked like after $3\frac{1}{2}$ months!).

an antifouling made specially for outboards and sterndrives: copper-based paints should be avoided at all costs, because they will accelerate corrosion of the aluminium lower unit.

The equipment required before going to sea in an outboard-powered boat has already been covered. But just as important as any equipment is the skipper's ability, more specifically his seamanship. Part of the attraction, as well as the danger, of boating at sea is that there are so many unpredictables! Usually the consequences turn out to be pleasant: unpleasant surprises are rare. But the best insurance against surprises, pleasant or unpleasant, is to learn about the unpredictables.

How can we best do that? First, know the waters you are using. Buy a chart of the area, and study it at leisure. Memorise where the dangers are, unmarked rocks, sand banks, perhaps even a wreck. Are there strong tides that will carry you off course? Spring tides give an unusually high rise and fall, reducing depths which may usually be safe. What is the weather forecast? Is the calm weather going to turn nasty in a few hours, before you get back to harbour? Is the fuel on board enough for the round trip? You need to allow a fuel reserve of at least 15% in case of bad weather or other delay.

It is the duty of the skipper to take all these factors into account before going to sea. If he has carried out the planning process properly and satisfied himself that it is safe to put to sea, the chances are that everyone on board will have a happy time—and that, after all, is the aim of pleasure boating!

Appendix A   Essential spares and tools

The spares and tools you carry on board should be adequate to allow first aid to the parts most likely to give trouble, rather than to effect a permanent repair to anything that could go wrong.

Some engine manufacturers provide a tool kit which in their opinion contains the basic tools required. This will normally consist of:

- plug wrench
- special screwdriver that converts for standard as well as cross-headed screws
- spanner(s) to remove the carburettor and fuel pump
- spanner(s) to remove the manual recoil starter
- pliers.

Basic spares likely to be included are:

- emergency starter rope
- set of spark plugs
- flushing attachment for the cooling system
- spare shear pins and split pins (if appropriate).

To these I would add:

- fuel filter element
- spare propeller
- propeller thrust washer
- kill switch lanyard
- spare ignition key (hidden)
- sharp boating knife
- spare propeller shaft nut, and the appropriate sized spanner
- spanner for transom nuts and bolts.

If you are going away on holiday, an additional spares kit consisting of fuel pump repair kit, water pump impeller and (if fitted) a set of points would prevent the outboard from being out of commission while you wait for parts. This would still only give you a very basic kit; but if the outboard needs to be dismantled, the repair will take a few days anyway, which will usually be sufficient time for the importer or distributor to send through the necessary parts.

Appendix B Winter service

The term winter service is somewhat misleading: more appropriate would be 'end-of-season' service, since it is important to carry it out before winter sets in. If you don't, it may be too late—turn to Chapter 5 to see why!

Your outboard owner's manual will give details of specific actions recommended for a particular engine type: here is a general list of the items that should be covered.

1. Flush the cooling system with fresh water.

2. Disconnect the fuel line and let the carburettor(s), so far as possible, run dry. During the last 10 seconds spray a storage oil through the carburettor venturi(s).

3. Service fuel filters.

4. Remove spark plug(s), squirt 10ml of outboard oil into the cylinders through the spark plug hole(s) and carburettor venturi(s), turning the engine over several times by rotating the flywheel: loosely replace the spark plug(s), and plug the carburettor venturi with an oily tissue.

5. Wash the outboard down with fresh water and spray the engine with WD40 or similar.

6. Remove and inspect the propeller, and if it is damaged, send it off for repair. Grease the shaft.

7. Even if you intend to leave the engine on the boat, disconnect and remove the battery, charge it and store in a cool dry place.

8. Check the sacrificial anode, and replace it if more than 50% used.

9. Lubricate all greasing points, grease all moving parts and cables, steering, shift and throttle.

10. Clean and grease the remote control box.

11. If the manual starter rope is cut or frayed, replace it.

12. Drain and replace gear oil.

13. Where applicable, check that the gearcase drain passage(s) are clear, using compressed air or a pipe cleaner.

14. Touch up any paint damage.

15. Drain portable fuel tank(s)—you can use the fuel up in your car, even if it is premix: the small amount of oil will not cause any damage. If the tank is metal, spray some WD40 into it and put on the cap. Disconnect the fuel line connector if fitted.

16. Drain and clean built-in fuel tanks.

17. Check fuel lines and other hoses for damage and replace if necessary.

18. At the start of the next season, the outboard can be recommissioned simply by refitting everything you have removed or loosened. Fit new spark plugs: cleaning them damages the porcelain glaze and encourages fouling.

Appendix C Submersion

Even with today's electrically complex outboards, submersion doesn't automatically mean disaster, provided that you ensure it is properly handled.

If you cannot get immediate technical assistance, it is better to leave the outboard underwater, until help can be organised. Corrosion is caused by damp metal reacting with air, so if the engine remains submerged, away from the air, it will come to less harm.

In the first hour after submersion corrosion will be slow, but thereafter every minute that the outboard remains untreated accelerates the damage.

If you wish (or have) to treat the outboard yourself following submersion, the steps to take are as follows:

1. Remove cowling and spark plugs. Disconnect fuel line if fitted.
2. Wash out the inside of the engine with clean fresh water, preferably with a hose, turning the engine over by hand so that all engine parts are thoroughly washed and cleaned of salt and silt.
3. Wash down the outside, including awkward places such as under the flywheel.
4. Wash out the inside of the engine with methylated spirits, turning it over by hand so that all engine parts are thoroughly coated with the alcohol, which will absorb water.
5. Squirt outboard oil into the engine via the carburettor and spark plug hole(s), rotating the engine with the manual starter or electric starter.
6. Add sufficient oil to the fuel tank to bring the fuel-oil ratio down to 10:1.
7. Connect the fuel line and press primer bulb repeatedly until the carburettor(s) overflow(s). This purges the fuel system of water.
8. Operate the starter, manual or electric, to remove excess oil from the cylinders.
9. Refit spark plug(s), plug cap(s) and kill switch key.
10. Switch on the ignition and operate the starter, and try to start the engine using choke if necessary.

11. If the engine doesn't start, refer to the trouble-shooting chart in your owner's manual and attempt to rectify the fault.

12. When the engine starts, keep it running at a fast idle (2000rpm) for half an hour, sufficient to ensure all the moisture has been driven out, and all bearing surfaces are coated with oil.

13. Take the outboard to a service dealer as soon as possible so that he can check it for damage likely to cause problems in future.

Appendix D Table of features

Use this table to decide the features you want on your outboard, then look for the brand that supplies your requirement.

Group	Feature	1	2	3	4	5	6	8	10	20	35	40	50	60	75	115	130	150	175	200	225	250	275	300
Motor	Electric	*	*	*	*	*																		
	Diesel											*	*											
	Four-stroke	*	*	*	*	*	*	*	*	*	*	*												
Ignition	Magneto	*																						
	Electronic		*	*	*	*	*	*	*	*	*	*	*	*	*	*	*	*	*	*	*	*	*	*
	Computer													*	*	*	*	*	*	*	*	*	*	*
Fuel	Premix	*	*	*	*	*	*	*	*	*	*	*												
	Injection																				*	*	*	
	Oil mixing	*	*	*	*	*	*	*	*	*	*	*	*	*	*	*	*	*	*	*	*	*	*	*
	Oil injection									*	*	*	*	*	*	*	*	*	*	*	*	*	*	
Starter	Manual	*	*	*	*	*	*	*	*	*	*	*												
	Manual & electric						*	*	*	*	*	*	*											
	Electric									*	*	*	*	*	*	*	*	*	*	*	*	*	*	*
Shaft length	Short	*	*	*	*	*	*	*	*	*	*	*	*	*										
	Long	*	*	*	*	*	*	*	*	*	*	*	*	*	*	*	*	*	*	*				
	Extra long					*	*	*	*	*						*	*	*	*	*	*	*	*	*
	Extra extra long																						*	*
Propeller	Conventional	*	*	*	*	*	*	*	*	*	*	*												
	Through hub exhaust						*	*	*	*	*	*	*	*	*	*	*	*	*	*	*	*	*	*
	High reverse thrust	*	*	*	*	*	*	*																
	Counter rotation																*	*	*	*	*	*	*	*
Shift	Forward	*																						
	Forward+neutral		*	*																				
	Forward+neutral+reverse				*	*	*	*	*	*	*	*	*	*	*	*	*	*	*	*	*	*	*	*
Miscellaneous	Clamp screws on bracket	*	*	*	*	*	*	*	*	*	*	*												
	Trim tab												*	*	*	*	*	*	*	*	*	*	*	*
	Power trim											*	*	*	*	*	*	*	*	*	*	*	*	*
	Power steering																			*	*	*	*	*
	Lighting coil/alternator			*	*	*	*	*	*	*	*	*	*	*	*	*	*	*	*	*	*	*	*	*
	Shallow water drive	*	*	*	*	*	*	*	*															
	Tiller handle	*	*	*	*	*	*	*	*	*	*	*	*	*										
	Engine monitor												*	*	*	*	*	*	*	*	*	*	*	*
	Voice message																				*			

Fig. 54. The features available at each level of power. Note that two-stroke engines are available throughout the size range.

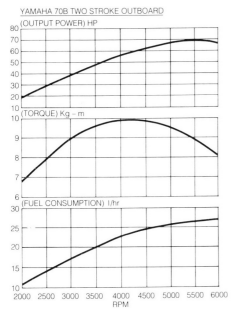

Fig. 55. Performance curve of the two-stroke Yamaha 70B petrol outboard.

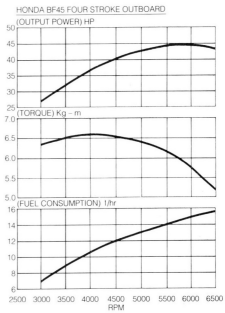

Fig. 56. Performance curve of the four-stroke Honda BF45 petrol outboard.

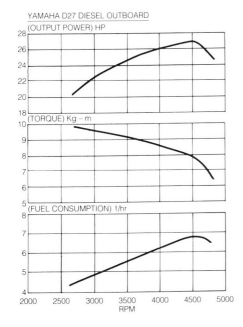

Fig. 57. Performance curve of the four-stroke Yanmar diesel outboard.

Fig. 58. Boat speed vs engine mounting height (long-shaft models).

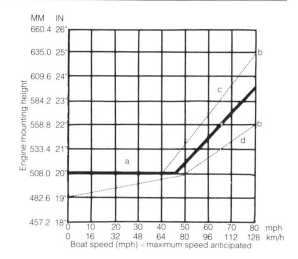

a *This solid line is recommended to determine the engine mounting height dimension.* Important: *Increasing the height of engine generally will provide the following:* 1) *less steering torque* 2) *more top speed* 3) *greater boat stability but* 4) *will cause more prop 'break loose' which may be noticeable when planing off or with a heavy load.*

b *These dotted lines represent the extremes of known successful engine mounting height dimensions.*

c *This line may be preferred to determine engine mounting height dimension if maximum speed is the only objective.*

d *This line may be preferred to determine engine mounting height dimension for dual engine installation.*

Appendix E   Useful addresses

Alphabetical list of principal outboard motor manufacturers or their main European headquarters:

British Seagull Ltd
Unit 3, Wessex Trade Centre
Ringwood Road
Poole
Dorset BH12 3PF
UK ,

Evinrude & Johnson:
OMC Europe NV
Pathoekweg 120
8000 Brugge
Belgium

Force, Mariner, & Mercury:
Marine Power Europe Inc
Parc Industriel de Petit-Rechain
4822 Verviers
Belgium

Honda Motor Europe Ltd
Caversham Bridge House
Waterman Place
Reading
Berkshire RG1 8DN
UK

Ruggerini Motori SpA
Via Cartesio 39
42100 Reggio Emilia
Italy

Selva SpA
Via Industria 13
23037 Tirano (Sondrio)
Italy

Suzuki Motor Company Ltd
Marine Division
Hamamatsu-Nishi
PO Box 1
432-91 Hamamatsu
Japan

Tomos
Tovarna Motornih Vozil,
Koper
Yugoslavia

Tohatsu Corporation
4-9, 3-chome
Azusawa
Itabashi-ku
Tokyo 174
Japan

Yamaha Motor Europe NV
Marine Division
PO Box 109
1420 AC Uithoorn
Netherlands

Yanmar Diesel Engine Co
Marine Department
Brugplein 11
1332 BS Almere
Netherlands

Here is a list of useful addresses, many of which are referred to in the text:

British Marine Industries Federation & ICOMIA:
Meadlake Place
Thorpe Lea Rd
Egham
Surrey TW20 8HE
UK

Finze Thrust Booster:
Fr.-Joh. Finze
Stader Landstrasse 32
2820 Bremen 77
Germany

Explosion-resistant fuel tanks:
E.P.Barrus Ltd
Launton Road
Bicester
Oxon OX6 0UR
UK

National Marine Manufacturers Association (NMMA)
600 Third Avenue
New York
NY 10016
USA

Royal Yachting Association (RYA)
RYA House
Romsey Road
Eastleigh
Hants SO5 4YA
UK

Technomarine AG
Seestrasse 50
CH-8802 Kilchberg-Zürich
Switzerland

Treysit vibration tachometer:
Treysit Presserei GmbH
Am Kalkhaus 5
3578 Treysa
Germany

Union Internationale Motonautique (UIM)
Stade Louis II Entrée H
MC 98000
Monaco

Index